P. W Hamer

From Ocean to Ocean

Being a Diary of a Three Months' Expedition From Liverpool to California

and Back

P. W Hamer

From Ocean to Ocean
Being a Diary of a Three Months' Expedition From Liverpool to California and Back

ISBN/EAN: 9783337010386

Printed in Europe, USA, Canada, Australia, Japan

Cover: Foto ©Andreas Hilbeck / pixelio.de

More available books at **www.hansebooks.com**

FROM OCEAN TO OCEAN.

FROM OCEAN TO OCEAN,

BEING

A DIARY OF A THREE MONTHS' EXPEDITION FROM

LIVERPOOL TO CALIFORNIA AND BACK,

FROM THE

ATLANTIC TO THE PACIFIC BY THE OVERLAND ROUTE.

"The world shall follow in the track we're going,
The Star of Empire glitters in the West."

𝔓rinted for 𝔓ribate ℭirculation.

1871.

LONDON:
PRINTED BY WILLIAM CLOWES AND SONS,
STAMFORD STREET AND CHARING CROSS.

WE dedicate this short diary of our very pleasant visit to those kind friends whom we have left behind us between the Oceans. Nothing can exceed such kindness and hospitality; and we feel that in a great measure we owe to their friendly aid those very pleasant impressions which will always be associated with our three months' journey from Ocean to Ocean.

THE AUTHORS.

S.S. "WISCONSIN,"
Off QUEENSTOWN,
27 *May*, 1871.

OCEAN TO OCEAN.

"A life on the ocean wave,
A home on the rolling deep,
Where the scattered waters rave,
And the winds their revels keep."

On the fifteenth day of March, in the present year of grace one thousand eight hundred and seventy-one, at three o'clock on a rough and stormy afternoon, we left the Liverpool landing-stage and went on board the Guion steamship "Colorado," Captain T. F. Freeman, bound for New York—bound for the West—the new and happy land.

We take permission to drop the curtain over the first twenty-four hours. The sea was méchant, and our fellow-passengers pretty much invisible; the sounds sometimes heard denoted a suffering which is neither confined to age nor sex.

The following day, passing down the Irish coast, we arrived about three in the afternoon off Queenstown, where we added some fifty or sixty forward passengers to the happy family of Irish and Germans already on board; after a short detention we steamed out of port, and before sunset were almost clear of the Irish land, standing well out to sea on the deep, *not* blue, Atlantic.

The "Colorado" is a fine steamship of 3000 tons burthen, 365 feet over all, built at Jarrow, roomy and comfortable; classed by sailors as one of the best sea-boats which at any time battled across the ocean.

We had not a very large party in the saloon, which is, perhaps, to be preferred to the overcrowded cabins in faster boats; but we had the advantage (as passengers) of an excellent brass band playing daily from ten to twelve, and who frequently favoured us with an evening entertainment. We retain a pleasant recollection of Mr. Emidy and his associates, wherever they may be.

Forward (after the first few days) we had a rather lively party of nearly nine hundred emigrants, coming from Ireland, from the Baltic, from Germany—from all over Europe; some to join their friends already settled there, others boldly to seek new fortunes in the home of the setting sun.

It may seem incredible, but statistics prove

that at this season of the year an average of one thousand emigrants leave Liverpool daily; and it is hardly to be wondered at when we consider that for ten or twelve days, at a cost of 6*l*., they are well-fed and conveyed from the overcrowded cities of the old world to a land where certain and well-paid employment awaits them, and where tenants are scarcer than farms.

We had few, if any, important incidents to mark the time. We had two zebras on board, objects of daily interest, who adapted themselves to circumstances uncommonly well. About half-way over we had to part with a valuable horse, which had got into trouble and rubbed its tail off during a very rough night. We celebrated the 21st March in a loyal manner, and our Captain drew up an address to the Marquis of Lorne, which was certified by the passengers, bottled, sealed, and sent overboard for the ocean post. In the middle of the Atlantic we experienced the benefit of a full gale of wind, and off the Banks we found ourselves involved in the usual fogs and snow-storms: head winds hindered us almost from land to land, but, pegging away, we fairly battled it out with old Father Neptune and beat him.

Passengers are a distinct study of human nature: the man who has "crossed before" engages his berth in advance, puts his luggage on board the previous day, comes lounging down to the wharf, in a soft hat, with a cigar in his mouth, selects a sheltered spot on deck, and watches with amusement the arrival of less experienced travellers and the endless confusion arising at the last moment from missing luggage, insatiable hack-men, and the often-repeated farewells from the wharf.

The middle-aged lady, resigned to any event, sits down on the first opportunity, and stops there; the younger members of her family are all excitement and curiosity. The Irish emigrant, jaunty as ever, with a shamrock in his hat and a short pipe in his mouth, comes on board apparently as careless as if he were leaving home for a fair. The lymphatic German quietly goes "below," and, if left alone, will probably sleep the voyage out in his boots from first to last. A large mixed party generally remain on deck from daylight to sunset, joking and smoking, determined to make the best of the voyage. Our Irishmen did not forget the 17th March, and have left a patch of bottles on the bottom of the Atlantic to mark the spot where they celebrated "Saint Patrick's day in the morning."

It would be impossible to speak too kindly of Captain Freeman's attention to the comfort of his passengers, or of the care with which advantage was taken of the sun, moon, and stars, at all times of the day and night: the temperature of the ocean, the movements of the glass, the water in the hold, the water in the tanks, the revolutions of the screw itself, were all most carefully and continually noted.

Mr. Yates, the head steward, has a wonderful secret in his recipe for mulled claret, and we wish our friend Charles (as he deserves) a better fortune than "the friendly law-suit" which deprived him of his property.

On Wednesday, the 29th, our pilot boarded us some two or three hundred miles from port, and the "City of Washington" coming up astern *put more jump* into our too-careful engineer, so that before midnight we had sighted the Highland lights; and when we turned out next morning we found ourselves safely anchored off Staten Island.

It is needless to speak of the handsome summer residences on Staten Island, of the beauty of the bay, or of the strength of the batteries protecting the entrance to the harbour, placed on opposite shores at a distance of barely two miles: it seems an impossibility for any hostile fleet to approach the City of New York. The bay at a very early hour was alive with large steam ferry-boats conveying passengers, carts, and carriages backwards and forwards in every direction.

At 9 A.M. we were clear of the doctor's visit, and went alongside the wharves, which are of wood, very poor and miserable, and quite unworthy of such important shipping interests.

We had very little trouble with the Customhouse people, and before noon we found ourselves comfortably settled at the Saint James's Hotel.

NEW YORK.

NEW YORK and its suburbs, forming a city of nearly 1,500,000 inhabitants, is so full of varieties, and, so to speak, of contradictions, that it is difficult, if not impossible, to give any general opinion about it: its size, wealth, and enterprise are undoubted; there are not finer residences to be found in any city than those of the Fifth Avenue and adjoining streets. Mr. Stewart's marble dry goods store, and the marble palace he has recently constructed as a residence, are magnificent. The churches are very numerous, handsome, and well filled; the parks are large, well laid-out and well cared for; you could not anywhere find a larger number of well-dressed people; the hotels for size, and their peculiar appointments, are unrivalled;—but, for all this, New York is not a finished city.

The wooden wharves at which you land are wretchedly poor and mean; the sidewalks in the business portions of the city, are badly paved and blocked up with cases, casks, and coals, and with the stalls of pea-nut and other vendors; the streets are cut to pieces by the rails for those wretched street cars;

the cab service is not regulated by authority, and the tariff ranges from 10*s*. to 20*s*. an hour, at the discretion of your driver, who gives you into the bargain all the style which may be derived from his fur-lined coat or velvet collar, supported by a large cigar in his mouth.

You notice everywhere in New York handsome warehouses, fine residences, and buildings which surprise you in so new a city. Private enterprise has done everything, but this city has been very much neglected by the public authorities, and beyond this, an unsettled, unfinished appearance arises from the very nature of events. In the United States every one wants to be "boss," nobody cares to take the back seat; the storekeepers all push for the best situations, the higher classes all desire to reside in the best quarter.

Trade prospers on the extravagant prices which are everywhere demanded, and as it prospers, so it advances itself, buying up residences and converting them into shops: the proprietors, bought out at fabulous prices, fall further back into the suburbs, or take to living out of town.

It was a positive sin to see Irishmen smashing in

handsome stone fronts, and wrecking good drawing-rooms, to make room for plate-glass windows and millinery. This sort of thing going on in every direction gives New York an unsettled, unfinished appearance.

But the great trouble of the city are the Irish, who, landing here, find themselves in such comfortable quarters that they do not care to move on to the West. There are more Irish in New York than in Dublin; and having monopolised they control the revenues and management of the city. Irishmen at home are distinguished for carelessness, want of system, and of forethought, and they have certainly muddled up the affairs of New York City to such a degree that New York people are themselves ashamed of it, and, sooner or later, must produce a Vigilance Committee to sweep Tammany out of office, and to regain the revenues so notoriously squandered and misapplied. The situation requires nerve, and the management of business men, who must for the moment put aside their own search after dollars, and do all they can to assist the citizens generally, in obtaining, as they now never can do, full value for their taxes.

The private residences and many of the shops have much the appearance of those in France or Belgium; the furniture of the hotels and houses of the better class is essentially French; cheap furniture is largely made from the black walnut wood of the country, which is excellent for that purpose.

The hotels in New York, and indeed everywhere in the United States, present to the traveller, previously accustomed only to European life, many interesting and amusing features.

The hotel generally occupies one entire block. The ground-floor is given up to one immense hall, in which you find establishments for the sale of cigars, newspapers, books, theatre and railway tickets; a long bar (generally very empty) for the supply of drinks; a general and very civilly managed intelligence office, with an immense safe; an unusually large barber's shop, served by black and white barbers, whose services are in constant request from six in the morning till six at night, and where you can always see a long row of men sitting in dentist's chairs reading the news, with their heads thrown back, and their feet thrown up to the same level. Going in rather bristly, they come out smooth as a looking-glass, with the exception of a heavy moustache.

In the hall itself you find groups of men sitting around in easy-chairs, others smoking and promenading incessantly, some using spittoons and some neglecting them.

The custom is to provide board and lodging at so much per diem, and for a charge of 12s. to 16s. you may order as frequently from the bill of fare for that day as you like. Many people seemed to find fault with this system, or rather to express a preference for plainer and better cooked food.

Upstairs these hotels are comfortably furnished and well kept, but in some of them, as everywhere else, the attendance is rather difficult to obtain, when you want it, and naturally troubles those who have occasion to catch the early trains. New York has very large and handsome churches. Quakers, Jews, Episcopalians, Presbyterians, Roman Catholics, Dissenters of every degree, coloured and uncoloured, all are cared for. At the churches which we attended the service was carefully and zealously carried through, the congregations large, well-dressed, and devout.

The entrance of the clergy and the choir was made in regular order, chanting from the vestry till they had occupied their appointed places in the church, and the service concluded in the same way, the congregation remaining seated till the choir and officiating clergymen had chanted themselves out of sight.

At Trinity Church on Easter Sunday we understood there were three hundred communicants at

7 A.M. We attended the second service, which was arranged at 10.30. We were fortunate enough to occupy, by invitation, the churchwardens' pew, for the church was thronged as soon as the doors were opened, and hundreds were turned away. The font and altar were profusely decked with white flowers, and the service was accompanied by two organs, about thirty choristers, and a full band of sixteen in the organ loft. The ceremony was impressive, and the flowers provided by church funds must have been very valuable: violets were selling that day at sixpence each, and the price of white rose-buds was from two shillings to four shillings a-piece in New York.

Clubs are becoming very general in this city; the Union is large, and well-appointed in every respect; and we "spent a very good time" at the monthly reception of the far-famed Century Club.

The roofs of most houses in the United States are flat and fire-proof, being covered with painted tin-plate. This material is said to be at once the strongest, cheapest, lightest, closest covering to be obtained, and all danger from leaking is now removed by the use of this same material, soldered by machinery into one "Continuous" water-proof sheet of any length.

Politics and newspaper-writing are quite a trade;

politicians receive a salary for their attendance in the Senate, and receive fees from such private individuals as require their services. This seems to be all wrong, and suggests the remedy of disqualifying at once and for future office all senators and congressmen, who can be shown to have accepted bribes.

Newspapers are in excess. Every city of two hundred people has its 'Gazette,' 'Banner,' 'Times,' or 'Journal,' with two columns containing the same day's news from Paris and London, two columns of jokes and local information, the balance in advertisements of an uninteresting character. The 'New York Herald,' and several similar papers, display extremely bad taste, in announcing deeds of crime, violence, and lawlessness in the largest type, discussing such subjects in a jocular spirit, as if it were a smart thing, and a good joke, to steal shares, and to defy the law, to shoot, plunder, and deceive.

Perhaps the greatest blot to be found on the United States is the little regard which is paid to human life, and the carelessness with which such crimes are regarded by the public generally, arising in a great degree from the uncertainty of the law. If such people as Mrs. Fair and others were acting under the knowledge that death would be the *certain* penalty for those who themselves destroyed life, there would be very few of such crimes, as those too frequently recorded; but so long as political interests corrupt judges, and "bogus" evidence and selected juries are allowed to influence such trials as these, then so long will there be a necessity for "back-pockets" and Vigilance Committees.

BOSTON.

STARTING from New York at 10.0 P.M. on Wednesday, the 5th of April, we travelled for the first time by sleeping-car. Ten minutes after going "on board" all hands had turned in, and we slept soundly till 6 A.M., when we were disturbed by the conductor announcing our arrival at "Borston."

Boston, the capital of the commonwealth of Massachusetts, otherwise "the Athens of America," otherwise the "Hub of the Universe," is one of the oldest cities in the Union. The stores present everywhere the appearance of a well-to-do, thriving city; the warehouses and public buildings are built of massive granite; the roads and streets are well kept, and present a favourable comparison with those of New York. Thursday happening to be the day set apart by the Governor, according to an old Puritan custom, for prayer and fasting, was kept as a general holiday, all the shops and offices being strictly closed. In the afternoon we went to see a base-ball match between the "Red Stockings" of Chicago and the Harvard University. The game was played on an enclosed ground, three thousand spectators being present. The fielding, particularly the way in which the ball was handled and returned, would have done any English cricket-ground credit; but the batting and bowling, so called, are very far behind cricket as we understand it. In the evening we went to hear Fechter in the "Lady of Lyons," at a large and handsome theatre. Good Friday, the following day, was not observed as a fast, and we spent it in visiting the outskirts of the city, which can boast of excellent roads, and country seats in every direction. "Boston Boxes," so called, are roomy, and handsomely built on well-timbered, rising ground, commanding fine views of the city and surrounding country.

The New England merchants are recognised in every market of the world as keen and shrewd adventurers; and it would be difficult to pay them a higher compliment than arises from the fact that the Jews cannot live in Boston.

In early times before the railroads, New England goods were peddled about in waggons from town to town, and to prevent competition with local interests, laws were passed imposing a heavy licence-fee on pedlars offering such goods for sale; but the New England clock-makers, equal to the occasion, evaded the tax by disposing of their clocks on a ninety-nine years' lease.

The irregular streets, and the style of architecture

in Boston, give it all the appearance of age, and remind the traveller more of Europe than any other city on the continent; and here we noticed, more than anywhere else, the played-out ideal Yankee, tall, with pale, thin face, dressed from top to toe in the blackest broad-cloth.

In appreciation of music, literature, the fine arts, for education and general refinement in society and manners, the Bostonians claim to be the first city of the Union. We offer no opinion on such a delicate subject.

The soil of Massachusetts is, as a rule, stony, poor, and difficult of cultivation. Nature has dealt hardly with the commonwealth in this respect. Spaniards, probably, would never have had the heart to settle here, and would have sailed away to warmer regions and a more generous soil; but not so the old Puritans. Made of sterner and better stuff, facing the difficulties of their situation, they have raised a city of which they may well be proud—the West may envy, but can never rival it—the massive granite streets of Boston will survive when the wooden buildings of Chicago have disappeared by fire, or as a result of time.

Boston is a city of large trade and of general wealth. The New England men, finding their country unequal to compete in the produce of corn, cotton, sugar, pork, or beef, with the warmer and more fertile States, have created a large trade in other natural products, such as ice, lumber, salt fish, and wooden ware; and they manufacture largely boots and shoes, cotton and woollen goods for consumption all over the Union, and even for export beyond the seas.

PHILADELPHIA.

On Monday, the tenth of May, we made the first real start on our journey from Ocean to Ocean, leaving New York in the morning, and travelling through a district where the farmhouses, barns, and fencing presented everywhere an appearance of prosperity and comfort, we arrived about noon at Philadelphia, the City of Brotherly Love. We were driven in an old-fashioned four-horse coach to the Continental Hotel, one of the largest and best-appointed establishments that we have visited in the country; and here, for the first time, we were introduced to coloured attendants, who certainly, whatever their faults, are better adapted for domestic service than the uncouth, slovenly Irish waiters so very general in the New York hotels.

We spent the afternoon in a very pleasant drive, visiting the Cemetery and Park. The latter comprises several hundred acres of beautiful land, situated on the banks overlooking the Delaware and the Susquehanah, well timbered with forest trees, and when completed will do credit to the city and to the gentlemen who have planned it, gratuitously giving their time as a committee of management.

The streets of Philadelphia, thronged with well-dressed and well-to-do citizens, and the fine stores of silversmiths, picture-dealers, and florists, impressed us very strongly with the wealth and importance of the second city of the Union. Chestnut Street, with its display of shawls, silks, and bonnets, is a perfect Vanity Fair for ladies.

The Cemetery is carefully laid out in close proximity to the city, with excellent roads. The white marble monuments, handsomely sculptured and well preserved, and the grounds tastefully arranged in the highest style of landscape-gardening, form an excellent example of that honour and respect for their dead which (as compared with other countries) is one of the most striking features of the country, and is to be noticed without exception in every part of the United States.

On the following day we visited the Girard College, the Prison, and other public buildings, all of which were models of order, neatness, and cleanliness, and well worthy of a Quaker city.

Philadelphia possesses an immense trade, and her influence in commercial matters almost rivals New York; her rivers are full of shipping from every country of the world, and her manufacturing interests are in advance of any city in the Union.

The streets are wide and mathematically regular;

the churches, which are numerous and beautiful, testify to the liberality and to the piety of the inhabitants; the markets are large, well arranged and well supplied; the houses of every class present an air of neatness and comfort, and it is said that, although comprising a much smaller population, Philadelphia contains actually more houses than the city of New York.

WASHINGTON.

"When Freedom, from her mountain height,
Unfurled her standard to the air,
She rent the azure robe of night,
And placed the stars of glory there."

LEAVING Philadelphia about nine P.M., another night in the sleeping-cars brought us early in the morning to Washington, in the district of Columbia, the well-known political capital of the United States.

The depôt, or railway station, is wretchedly mean, and the immediate neighbourhood about as unfinished and unsettled as is to be found in any of the western towns. This gives a bad impression to the stranger, and is altogether unworthy of the place.

We drove to Willard's hotel, and after breakfast visited the Treasury, Patent Office, Post-office, and several other public buildings. These massive structures, built of white marble, are so well known as to require no detailed description. The reader should imagine eight or ten splendid buildings similar in size and character to Saint George's Hall, Liverpool, built of pure white marble, scattered about a country town;

and this is the best idea we can give of Washington to the English mind. It would certainly have added to the public convenience if these immense buildings had been placed nearer together than at distances varying from one to three miles; and the unequalled effect such a group of buildings would have presented, increases the wonder why such arrangements were permitted.

We next visited the Capitol itself, and were fortunate enough to find both Houses sitting. This building, also of white marble, is surmounted by an immense dome, above which is a figure representing the noble Indian. The proportions of the Capitol are so large as to afford space for the Supreme Court and for both Houses of the Legislature. Approaching by a flight of steep marble steps, we entered a large circular hall beneath the dome, adorned with frescoes representing Indian and Spanish subjects of early history, and we were called upon to notice paintings representing the surrender of several English swords.

The Upper House, or Senate, were discussing the Ku Klux question; a bill having been introduced to repress, by military power, this organization which is supposed to exist in North Carolina: the object of such organization being to obtain an increase of political power by controlling the negro vote. However that may be, it appears certain that bands of armed white men disguised in black masks, were nightly patrolling, the country, looting, shooting, and frequently burning down the property of such coloured men as were not prepared to surrender their freedom, and to vote a "straight" Democratic ticket.

The members, who were each provided with an easy chair, writing-table and spittoon, were sleepily listening to a written speech from Mr. Salisbury, of Delaware, who was opposing the Ku Klux Bill. Presently, however, the hon. member threw down his papers, and with great energy denounced the promoters of the Bill, asserting that the whole affair was a conspiracy arranged with a view to the reintroduction of military rule in the South; affirming that all this trouble had been caused by men sent down purposely from the North, whom he described as "carpet baggers;" men bankrupt in fortune, destitute of resources; comparing them to worms which feed upon corruption, and to the vampire sucking the life-blood in the night chamber of the sleeping victim, and finished off by branding them as the most contemptible creatures whom God ever made.

In the Lower House, or Congress, we found them rather warmly discussing the propriety of appropriating dollars obtained under one estimate to some altogether different purpose. General Butler was pointed out to us, and also two of the coloured senators, who, in dress and conversation, seemed to hold their own at all events.

We found no particular interest in the business progressing in the Supreme Court, and left regretting that we could not photograph the Lord Chancellor reclining in an easy chair, rather rough about the hair, with his head thrown back, and a long lead pencil pointing upwards from his mouth.

We were told the following story about the brother of Mr. Salisbury, who was not celebrated for sobriety, taking his seat, and addressing the House *after* he had ceased to be a member. Some newspaper of the following day reporting this incident, and referring to a funeral in Indiana at which some one present had, at an awkward moment, ventured the observation that it was "a very quiet corpse," regretted that Mr. Salisbury was not content to remain "a quiet corpse," observing that, e'en in his ashes lived his wonted *fire-waters*.

Leaving Washington late in the afternoon of Wednesday, the twelfth of April, we arrived the same evening at Baltimore, the capital of Maryland.

BALTIMORE.

*" The despot's heel is on thy shore,
Oh, Maryland! my Maryland!"*

BALTIMORE has neither the bustle of New York, nor the old-fashioned look of Boston, nor the quiet, settled appearance of Philadelphia, but is a lively, pleasant city; the streets are clean, well paved, and carefully planted, and present very much the appearance of a prosperous seaport town: amongst its numerous churches there are several which are very handsome, and which have been built at the expense of private individuals.

Baltimore is celebrated all over the world for its beautiful women. Our visit was a short one, but we have certainly no reason to dispute the verdict.

The packing establishments of this city are the most extensive in the world, and fabulous quantities of peaches, oysters, and tomatoes are yearly packed for export. The oysters which we tasted on board the boats we concluded to be the finest which we had met with in this land of oysters. We visited a packing establishment, and were kindly shown the process by which oysters, delivered by the cartload, are measured and hoisted in iron baskets to an upper floor, and dipped into a tank of hot water, which opens them; they are then picked over by girls and passed on to women, who place them in cans. The whole operation from a live to a canned oyster occupied scarcely as much time as it takes to describe the operation. The shells when burnt form excellent lime.

Baltimore has a large and naturally-handsome park, purchased and supported by an extra cent charged on the fare to every passenger travelling in the street cars.

Chesapeake Bay is the noted resort of the canvas-back duck, and it may be interesting to those who advocate the abolition of English game laws to know that all the best ground is already rented and strictly protected.

We must award to Baltimore—at least, to the gentlemen residing at our hotel—credit for the most general indulgence in the habit which is peculiar to this continent and to seafaring people. We should be unwilling, in "a free country," to dispute a right to the free use of tobacco; but then, why not as freely use the full-sized spittoons so liberally provided? It seems hardly fair that those who do not share the enjoyment should be forced (whenever they cross the hall) to suffer from the too-unpleasant results of indulgence in " Solace " and " Morning glory."

PITTSBURGH.

We left Baltimore on Friday night, and found ourselves early next day crossing the Alleghany Mountains over an excellent railroad and through the finest scenery we had yet seen; the well-timbered mountains, the sheltered valleys, the blue smoke curling up from the comfortable farmhouses, and the thickets of rhododendron bordering every river and stream, witnessed at an altitude of 5000 feet above the sea, completed a scene which we passed from with regret.

We arrived at Pittsburgh about eleven, and found very little of interest to detain us. This city, favourably situated at the junction of the Monongahela and Alleghany with the Ohio, forms the manufacturing centre of Pennsylvania, so rich in coal and iron. Here they produce pig-iron, ship plates, sheet iron, boiler plate, glass and steel, brass and copper, in sheets and rods, and continue such manufacture to the details of smaller articles produced from such material.

' The city has been built up all around these works,

and, as a consequence, soot and smoke prevent any attention to appearances, and the city in this respect suffers from the enterprise which creates its wealth.

CINCINNATI.

We left Pittsburgh in the afternoon, and arrived early next morning at Cincinnati on the Ohio River.

The city itself is substantially built; the hotels, public buildings, and dry goods stores are the pride of the State of Ohio; and they claim that the bridge crossing to Covington, in Kentucky, is the finest to be found in any part of the country.

The outskirts of the city possess many beautiful private residences; the undulating country and the well-timbered hills are features very rarely to be met with in Western cities. No expense has been spared in the arrangements of the cemetery, and the landscape-gardening, water, trees and shrubs, give the appearance of very well-kept private grounds.

Cincinnati produces excellent wine, and has been christened "Porkopolis" from its large trade in pork.

These unhappy hogs are compelled to mount to their own destruction, which occurs at a height of thirty feet from the ground, and sliding down by their own weight from the top to the bottom of the factory, they are treated in the usual manner, and meeting a different reception at every stage of their progress they are eventually converted from living hogs to barrelled pork " inside of five minutes."

CHICAGO.

From Cincinnati we passed on in twelve hours to Chicago, the Queen of the West, the City of the lakes, possessing, as all the world knows, a fabulous trade in " passing on " the pork and grain produced in this section of the New World to the hungry, eager mouths awaiting such supplies in Europe. The warehouses and principal streets are handsome, and equal to New York itself; but the houses of the labouring classes are built of wood, and poor to the last degree.

Chicago has all the appearance of what it is—a large trading centre; the streets are everywhere on a dead level, and run in a straight line miles and miles away from the lake to the prairie.

We stopped at the Sherman House, an immense stone building, formerly raised six feet all round to bring it up to the level of the new street—the hotel being occupied during the alteration.

Eleven different railways centre at Chicago, bringing the produce of the North-Western States to this their most important market.

OMAHA.

"To the west, to the west, to the land of the free,
Where the mighty Missouri rolls down to the sea."

LEAVING Chicago on Tuesday, the eighteenth, we passed down through the States of Illinois and Iowa, crossing the Misissippi River at Clinton, and arrived at Council Bluffs on the Missouri on the morning of Thursday, the 20th of April.

The country through which we passed at first was thoroughly settled, and, apparently, well adapted for agriculture, the soil on every side as black as your hat; and some farmers of the district, joining the train, gave us fabulous accounts of heavy crops, and of corn growing fourteen feet in height. But it was evident as we passed along, from the nature of the villages, farmhouses, barns, and fencing, that we were getting farther and farther from civilization, and approaching the boundaries of the so-called Desert.

At Council Bluffs, or, rather, on the banks of the Missouri, three miles beyond that place, we met with our first and only check—a gale of wind was blowing so furiously, that the Captain of the steamer appointed to carry us across the Big Muddy, was unwilling to risk the voyage; there was so much top gear, on a very flat-bottomed basis, that the chances were we should get capsized, or banged against the stone piers of the bridge then building. The boat had been prevented by the gale from crossing the previous day, so that there were altogether nearly six hundred passengers crowding in the cabin; and here we stopped for nearly two hours; but there was not the slightest sign of impatience, every one in silence seemed contented to smoke, and spit, and wait. But one of us happening to overhear an arrangement proposed by the Captain, to put one hundred and fifty passengers out in the bows to steady her, and then "to chance it," we determined to give somebody else our chance, and we stepped off with the intention of sleeping at Council Bluffs; however, influenced by the advice of a friend who was determined "to strike" Brigham for Sunday, we went on board the ferry, a smaller boat, and after a further detention of two hours, we were taken up instead of down the river, and with three or four bumps, and once aground, we were landed on a sandbank and conveyed in carriages to the Omaha depôt. The luggage following in waggons "got mired up," and completed a delay of nearly six hours.

There is supposed to be consolation in everything. We consoled ourselves, that we were not quite so badly off as a bride and bridegroom, married that morning at Council Bluffs, making such a wretched start on their journey in life: they subsequently joined our train, and spent the next two days and nights in the cars between Omaha and Denver.

OMAHA TO SALT LAKE.

However, about 4 P.M. we were all on board again, and soon left Omaha behind us, rattling along at a splendid pace, to make up for our lost time.

The next morning found us well out on the plains, sandy and brown, in places hardly covered with dry straggling grass; antelopes now and then in sight, sometimes a river or creek, and a few wild ducks, to vary the monotony; but the total absence of stock, fencing, or houses, made us sensible that at last we were quite alone in the wilderness.

The following day we found ourselves in a country covered with sage-brush, and white with alkali, inhabited only by prairie dogs and Indians, stopping every now and then for water and wood, and three or four times daily for meals, at "Cities" containing from twenty to thirty wooden buildings crowded together, as if every inch was an object in a country unoccupied for several hundred miles on each side of them. Most of the inhabitants made a point of being on hand when the train arrived, and gave us a very fair idea of what is understood by a "hard set" of men. The large and numerous saloons and "sample rooms" seemed to indicate that here, as elsewhere, human nature is regulated by the inevitable laws of supply and demand.

The meals so called, with a few exceptions as at Cheyenne, where "square meals" are provided in comfortable airy rooms with decent attendance, are provided in mean wooden buildings adjoining the depôt. On long tables, covered with dirty cloths, where greasy tough meat, a liquid called coffee, potatoes, and sometimes eggs are dashed down—sometimes by white men, sometimes by coloured servants or Chinamen, sometimes by gaudily-attired females—we doubt if hunger itself is a sufficient sauce to give any one a relish for *that* kind of food.

However, we were glad to know that we were comparatively safe and well off in these cities as compared with the early history of the line. Then Laramie was a "rough place," as our conductor told us; Bryan was a "hard place;" Jules Burgh was the roughest place you ever saw. The men who constructed the line were followed up from point to point by men and women of the most abandoned class, and drinking, gambling, and shooting, made these places about as bad as bad could be.

We were timed to arrive about 6 P.M. for breakfast, 12 for dinner, 4 for tea, 7 for supper: the charge being one dollar for each meal, which does not vary except in the degree of discomfort.

At nearly every station can be seen mounds of earth denoting the remains of men who had been removed by a violent death. At Jules Burgh seventeen men were hung in one morning by the Vigilance Committee. At Bryan they would shoot you if you didn't look pleasant. At Laramie a visitor at the breakfast-table was shot for taking too much gravy. In Virginia City men were accustomed to shoot somebody when they had a fancy to get a name up. At Los Agelos a man was shot across the street by an entire stranger, for luck; and only the other day a case is reported at Montana when a miner, not waiting for a reply from a stranger, to the strange inquiry of "how he would have it," rather hurriedly made his own choice, and shot him through the head.

Life seems in these early times to have been of little value: free shooting is certainly an established institution of this free country.

Outside of States, and even of Territories, it will be understood that the laws are powerless to control such men, but when matters reach a crisis a Vigilance Committee is formed, and a very sudden death awaits prisoners who are brought to *that* tribunal. It was a satisfaction to hear, as we did from a gentleman connected with the mail service, that he did not know of one instance out of twenty or more where men who, having themselves taken life, had been allowed to "die with their boots off;" an expression referring to such of them as have been either hanged or shot.

By Saturday we were tired of the plains and alkali, but in the afternoon, the country entirely changed its character, and, travelling through splendid mountain scenery, we passed the gorges known as the Weber and Echo canyans, and entered the outskirts of the Mormon settlement.

The line subsequently passed through a valley containing small farms and cultivated land for a distance of fourteen miles, and we arrived about 5 P.M. at Ogden, the terminus of the Union Pacific, the depôt of the Central Pacific, and the junction for Salt Lake City.

Leaving Ogden again in an hour a well-appointed Mormon train carried us over a good road, at a fairish pace, to Utah, or Salt Lake City, where we arrived about 8 P.M.

SALT LAKE.

THE City of the Saints was very full of Gentiles that evening, and we had some difficulty in obtaining rooms. However, after some trouble, we settled down into comfortable quarters at the Townshend House, so called from Mr. Townshend, the proprietor, one of the leading Mormons.

We visited the theatre the same evening, and found it well filled with Saints and Gentiles, and we noticed a general absence of distinguished appearance. A French actress was entertaining the house, with ideas rather different from those which might have been expected in the City of the Saints.

The City Recorder, sitting next to us, was good enough to point out the families of the elders, conspicuous generally for their numbers and for a better style of dress. The elders themselves, who occupied rocking chairs, seemed to prefer the society of the younger ladies of the party.

On Sunday we visited the Temple, and found a large congregation of nearly two thousand homely-dressed people assembled.

During the service the sacrament was administered without a pause or any particular cessation for this purpose. The congregation helped themselves from large white jugs of water and plated cake-baskets full of bread, which were handed round by shabbily-dressed men at one period of the service.

The Mormons are very much "exercised" over the deposits of silver and lead which are almost daily being discovered in their mountains; and Gentiles are pouring in so rapidly, it seems very probable that before long the Mormons will be outnumbered, and outvoted, when, as a consequence, the system will be broken down or "played out." The city is well planned and well managed, and reflects much credit on Brigham Young and his confederates. Whatever may be passing *inside* the neat wooden houses, outside, at least, they have every appearance of prosperity and comfort. Almost without exception every house possessed an ample garden and an orchard of peach-trees. The streets were full of teams loading and unloading, to and from the mines. Brigham Young is considered to be very wealthy, his income being derived from tithes; the regulation being that one-tenth of all produce should be surrendered to the head of the Church. When the hen lays ten eggs, put one aside for Brigham. As a sign of the times, we were informed that Judge M'Kean was zealously and fearlessly enforcing the laws of the United States, which have hitherto been disregarded; and great credit must be given to Bishop Tuttle for the handsome episcopal church, which has been constructed at a cost of thirty thousand dollars; and for the Sunday-schools, which have already an attendance of more than two hundred pupils.

OGDEN TO SAN FRANCISCO.

We left the Salt Lake City at four o'clock on the afternoon of Monday, the twenty-fourth, and travelling all the following day across dreary deserts of sand and sage-brush, we arrived very early on Wednesday morning at the summit of the Nevadas, clothed in pine-trees and perpetual snow.

This change of scenery was exciting and invigorating. The ascent to the Nevadas is made over a line of railway covered in with forty miles of snowsheds; but the descent we made in an open observation-car, amidst scenery of the grandest description. Almost in the very clouds, gigantic pines and snow-clad rocks towered above and around us, while beneath us rivers rolled in valleys at a depth of 1500 feet. The eye noticed everywhere a total absence of civilization—nothing but nature in all her grandeur.

On the slopes of the Nevadas we passed out of the pine-trees into a rolling country, dotted with oaks and forest-trees, bearing at many points evidences of the untiring search for gold, and again passing out of the timber, we found ourselves at last in happy, sunny California.

Wide plains stretched away on every side of us, rich with grass, dotted with cattle, studded with oak-trees of immense size, having all the appearance of an English park. A bright sun and abundance of summer flowers completed the picture—a most striking contrast to the dreary country we had left behind us.

At midday " we made " the city of Sacramento, and the rest of our journey, was through cultivated plains, in which the corn was already far advanced, as in our English July. The substantial depôts, villages, and large farm buildings, plainly showed the prosperity of the settlers. At six P.M. we reached Oakland, the terminus of the Central Pacific, distant twenty miles by water from the city of San Francisco, and the last station on our journey from Ocean to Ocean.

CALIFORNIA.

CALIFORNIA is the finest State in the Union, and San Francisco is anything but a one-horse place "you bet." At Sacramento we found a telegram welcoming us to California; we were met at Oakland and taken over to rooms engaged for us at the Grand Hotel in San Francisco; and so it went on from first to last. If you wish to please a Californian, allow him to do everything, and to pay for everything; if you wish to insult him, "hit out" for yourself.

San Francisco, or "Frisco," would be classed as a fine city wherever good houses, hotels and shops, and handsome public buildings are counted in. The bay is sufficiently large and safe to float the combined navies of the world. The city, at first built on the shores of the bay, has been pushed outwards into the water by means of pile-driving, and pushed backwards into the country, by the removal of the sand-hills, which are scooped up with a dredging machine worked on a railroad, which machine empties the sand into the trams, which are carried away for tipping, and thus continuous level streets are obtained in situations formerly a mere waste of sand-hills.

The city of San Francisco, and the citizens, present

to the stranger an appearance of general ease, and seem, so to speak, to be rolling in luxury and wealth. An open-handed, liberal spirit extends itself beyond private individuals, to the hotels and shops. The country settler takes you out of town and keeps you there, afterwards passing you on to his neighbours, who entertain you, and again pass you on to their neighbours, so that you soon get introduced and entertained by the whole country-side. We were told that Mr. Ralston, manager of the Bank of California, frequently entertained a hundred guests, providing them with a train to his place near Santa Clara, conveying them in his own carriages from the depôt, and providing sleeping accommodation, in addition to princely entertainment, for so large a party.

At the hotels and restaurants a "free lunch," and "free supper," is always provided on a sideboard ready for all comers: ham and lobsters, sirloin and trotters, shrimps, cheese, and crackers, are very much at the service of such individuals as have business with "the man in the white coat."

We do not hesitate to say that, so far as our experience goes, the accommodation which the Grand Hotel provides is unsurpassed anywhere: large and handsome outside, inside you find every convenience and comfort which civilization can supply. There are few places in this wide world where eighteen shillings a-day enables you to live in a Palace, provides you with an excellent bedroom, and entitles you to order as much or as little food as you please, from six A.M. to twelve P.M. We append a bill of fare, to avoid the appearance of romancing; and we ask where else for the same money, you can breakfast on broiled salmon, young chickens and strawberries, and dine in a banqueting hall from a menu including turtle-soup, salmon, sturgeon, venison, ices, and fruit?

The markets of San Francisco are large, well kept, and abundantly supplied with fruit, flowers, fish, poultry, &c., selling at the following prices: hams, 2s., butter, 1s. 6d., strawberries, 5 cents, salmon, 8 cents, sturgeon, 6 cents, lamb, beef, venison, for less than 1s. per pound. There seemed to us, from the supply, to be an unusually large demand for pickles, which were sold out of large wooden casks.

Gold and silver, by general consent, are the only legal tender in California: you can exchange greenbacks at the money-dealers of course, but nobody uses them. It was very comfortable to feel gold again, and to get large twenty-dollar pieces, value of four pounds, in exchange for the too-well circulated currency of the East.

The weather during our visit was very pleasant; a

warm sun, not too hot, with a cool breeze from the Pacific. We had left New York with the trees just breaking into leaf, to find winter and ice at Boston, full spring in Baltimore, winter again at Pittsburgh, early spring at Chicago, several feet of snow on the Nevadas; but in California it was midsummer, as the fruit, flowers, trees, and corn-fields plainly told us. The year is made up in this country, by ten months of summer and two months of rain, when the settlers come into the city for the season. Perhaps so much sun may have influenced the habits and customs of California.

They produce excellent wines and brandy from Californian grapes, and perhaps it is quite as well to meet the demand for "morning smiles" and other pleasantries. They seem to be more particular here than in the East as to how they take it; no tin mugs are used here to smash and froth up everything: in this country drinks are served by well-shaved, pleasant-looking men, dressed in very white linen from head to foot, who carefully arrange the proportions, mixing them with a spoon, completing them with a piece of pine-apple or a strawberry, or a leaf of fresh mint; placing before you, in a silver dish, olives, cloves, peppercorns, coffee berries, and spice, to remove the taste or prepare you for another effort. They certainly understand this business on the Pacific coast. If any difference arises between friends as to who shall settle for the drinks, the man in the white coat quietly, unasked, hands over the dice-box to settle the question. Fruit of most kinds is abundant; pears, apples, tomatoes, and peaches are largely canned for export. At a ranche we visited, thirty acres of strawberries were under cultivation, and a ton of ripe fruit had the same morning been sent to market; a neighbour was planting seven hundred acres of almonds, and all the ranches, possess fruit orchards, of a size unusual anywhere out of the Golden State.

Trade thrives in California, but the merchants have invented a new complaint; they say that the facilities of transit are against them; in former years they could buy up stocks, and control an article for six months certain, but now Chicago can come to the rescue in six days by rail. No doubt the line of steamers they have to China, will open up a very large market, for anything suitable they can find to send there. Money finds ready employment at ten to twelve per cent. per annum on good security; formerly, they jokingly tell you, it was one per cent. a minute.

There is a large Chinese population in California, and different opinions are expressed as to the value, or otherwise, of such labour; they are certainly clean, steady, quiet, and industrious, and for such work as strawberry-picking by contract, and garden cultivation generally, they are invaluable. Chinamen are exclusively employed in maintaining five hundred miles of the Central Pacific road, but the Irish detest them for working too cheap, and people in trade complain that they buy nothing: they live on rice and fish, and send home the balance of their wages to China; either to their parents, to whom, by Chinese laws, it legally belongs, or with a view to the happy time, when they shall once more return to the land of their fathers. Our host told us that, last season, some Irishmen, watching an opportunity, burnt down his Chinese barracks, destroying all that they possessed.

They tell you in San Francisco that the honest miner is played out: however that may be, very large quantities of gold and silver, silver lead, and quicksilver, from somewhere or another, contribute very materially to the welfare of the place.

Wheat is largely grown on the Pacific coast; sometimes ten thousand acres in one patch without a hedge. The climate suits the grain, which ripens quickly, producing very white flour and very little bran. They reap in some places with a machine, which cuts off the ears only, threshing and winnowing it at one operation; and frequently the land is only ploughed up once for two seasons; the grain which falls from one crop remaining uninjured on the dry soil till the rainy season arrives, when it takes root and produces a "volunteer crop" of fair average quantity.

Game seemed abundant. We saw quails, snipes, ducks, and plenty of hares, squatting about outside the corn lands, very much as if they were well looked after by keepers, which of course they are not.

We must not forget the Cliff House and the seals, although they will soon be as well known as Stewart's store in New York. We were trotted out very fast and comfortably some eight miles one beautiful afternoon, to find a capital hotel built on the cliffs, overhanging and overlooking the Pacific, and sitting in the sunny verandah, carefully "fixed off" by the man in the white coat, we had a beautiful view of the blue Pacific, the Golden gates, and the rocky coast. On the rocks in front of us, within rifle-shot, were hundreds of large seals sleeping, splashing, sunning themselves, sprawling in and out of the water, and "hobbing around the rocks." San Francisco is very proud of these seals, and a heavy fine would be enforced for shooting them.

After leaving the Cliff House, we drove along the beach, and when our friend sent his horses knee-deep into the breakers, we felt that we had very fairly completed our journey from the Atlantic to the Pacific, from "Ocean to Ocean."

If we were asked to give an opinion as to the best country to settle in, we should without hesitation pronounce for California. The West has its advantages, but generally the population outside of the cities is hard and rough, the climate uncertain and cold. Here you have fine soil, and well timbered; ten months of summer; fruit—of all kinds--at discretion; game in abundance; farms at a moderate price; friendly, hospitable, and liberal neighbours; a metropolis supplying everything which the world itself supplies, from the Italian opera to London pickles; news of the same day from London and Paris; seven days from New York, sixteen days from London, twenty-one days from China —where, in this world, if a man means to move, can he find a better home than this?

A CALIFORNIAN RANCHE.

"A ranche," so called by the Spaniards, and perpetuated by the Californians, who prefer to keep all the Spanish names they can, is a country-house establishment, and may be well described from a visit we made. Leaving San Francisco early one morning, we went by rail to Santa Clara, where we were met at the station, by a light four-wheel buggy and a team (there are no one-horse traps on this side of the Nevada, everybody drives two or nothing), and travelling over two miles of fair road, we arrived at the entrance to our friend's property. Approaching from the main road, by an avenue of nearly a mile, we came up to a comfortable, open-doored, green-windowed, white-painted, wooden house, under the shade of large trees, surrounded by lawn, flowers, and flower-garden, close to a lake formed from a running stream passing in and out of it; the stabling and coach-houses a hundred yards away on the bank of the stream, adjoining the flower-garden. Thirty acres of black loamy soil, irrigated by artesian wells, was under cultivation as an orchard; strawberries below, and above them peaches, cherries, apples, pears, almonds, quinces, all in full bearing, most carefully looked after by Chinamen, who seemed to be handling the strawberries very carefully, working by contract under a boss, also a Chinaman; by an excellent system, saving time and strawberries.

Beyond the orchard were several hundred acres of land under grain crops, and grass paddocks; closer to the house, paddocks and shedding for trotting horses, and a gravelled race track of half a mile to time the trotters. A dairy with a herd of well-bred cows completed the establishment, of which our host was very proud.

We have purposely refrained from all reference to

social matters in our diary, and this alone prevents our referring to the kindness and hospitality with which we were entertained at the ranche.

Happy is the property which has only one drawback! George Robins complained of the litter from the rose leaves; our hostess complained of damage to her lawn from the trespassing of the wild ducks.

SAN FRANCISCO TO DENVER AND SAINT LOUIS.

We left San Francisco with much regret on Monday, May the first, and crossing to Oakland at eight A.M., we were soon once more on board the cars, heading for the East, homeward bound.

Before evening we had left behind us the fertile sunny plains; at supper-time we were once more in the mountains, and the sun went down in the majestic pine forests, which clothe the entire summit of the Nevadas, adding to the beauty of a scene which no pen can describe.

Travelling for the next forty-eight hours over the plains, which seemed to us even more dreary and dusty than on the outward voyage, we reached "Cheyenne" about noon on Thursday, where we "stepped off," and leaving the line of the Union Pacific, we entered the cars of the Denver Pacific Railroad, and were soon bowling along over the plains for Denver: we were fortunate in finding one of the drawing-room cars attached, and getting away from the dust, heat, and alkali, we very much appreciated the rolling, pleasant plains of Colorado through which we passed. We noticed settlements springing up at many of the stations along the line, and there seems a prospect that this part of the country will soon be settled up. The line at this point runs parallel, at a distance of thirty miles, to the ranges of the Rocky Mountains, which we now saw for the first time; as although on the Union Pacific we had reached an elevation of 8,000 feet, the ascent was so gradual, and the country so anything but rocky, that, without information, you might suppose yourself travelling over the plains.

We reached Denver about sunset the same day, and, much to our surprise, found it to be quite a large and substantial town: excellent stores, large hotels, well-formed streets, and handsome well-horsed carriages, seemed to show that the capital of Colorado has passed through the troubles of its early history, and is likely to become an important and wealthy city.

Denver, as is well known, is the centre of important gold and silver mining interests, and we had here the opportunity of meeting with some of the miners and pioneers, who had come to town to attend an acrobatic exhibition, at that time visiting the place. We feel freer now to make observations respecting these gentlemen than at that time, judging from appearances, and from the reputation which they possess as free shooters. We refer those who may be interested in the future of Denver and Colorado, to the following extract from a pamphlet edited by Mr. Gilpin, Governor of this State:

"Hence have already come these new States from this other seaboard, and the renewed vivacity of progress with which the general heart palpitates.

"Will this cease or slacken? Has the grass obliterated the trails down the Alleghanies or across the Mississippi? Rather let him who doubts seat himself upon the bank of the supreme Missouri River and await the running dry of his yellow waters. For sooner shall he see this than a cessation in the crowd, now flowing loose to the western seaboard! Gold is dug, lumber is manufactured, pastoral and arable agriculture grow apace. A marine flashes into existence, commerce resounds, the fisheries are prosecuted, vessels are built, steam pants through all the waters. Each interest stimulating all the rest, and perpetually creating novelties, a career is commenced to which, as it glances across the Pacific, the human eye assigns no turn!"

"It is to the infallible judgments, and the intrepid valour of the pioneers, that the American people owe the selection of Colorado, and the auspicious metropolitan site of Denver. The one crowns and embraces the supreme altitude of the Continent, and majestically arches the Cordillera, the other rests in the focus of the continental scheme, of activity and fresh forces. By their exalted energy and devotion, the imperilled Union has been saved from obscure speculations and blind theories."

There was a rumour at the hotel in the evening that the line of the Kansas Pacific, over which we were about to travel to Kansas City, had been attacked the previous day by Indians; but we decided to persevere, and left again about 9 P.M. The next day was certainly the pleasantest and most interesting of our journey across the plains, and we strongly recommend this change of route, to any one travelling to or from California. In our drawing-room car we travelled along; undulating fertile plains (similar in appearance to the downs at Epsom) stretched far away on every side into space, uncultivated and untouched. Here and there rivers, bordered with forest trees, and frequent herds of antelope, disturbed by our train, galloped over the plains, and seemed to race with us for miles, as we passed along over their self-selected feeding-grounds.

We noticed frequent skeletons of buffalo on the plains, and at Kit Carson we entered the real buffalo country. At first we saw them in groups of twenty or thirty, feeding far away in the distance; then these groups became larger and more frequent, and finally we ran up to a herd of probably several hundred, passing within a hundred yards of them—so close, indeed, that several rifle shots were fired at them by the conductors in the baggage cars. We saw buffalo off and on for a period of four hours. It was a wonderful sight, as we rolled along, sitting comfortably on the sofas of these luxurious cars, to push up the windows and to watch these herds quietly grazing on the uncultivated, untrodden prairie; and it was with regret we noticed many skeletons everywhere dotting the plains, intimating too plainly that before many years have passed away the buffaloes will have disappeared; for numerous as they are in this section to-day, the constant destruction of these noble animals —sometimes by Indians and settlers, for food, but more frequently for the sake of the tongue and robe, and often for the mere wanton sport of killing them— must very shortly drive them "back and back," till, finally, they will be blotted out of existence and only remain in the history of the past.

We had previously frequently dined and breakfasted on antelope meat, which is tender and excellent; to-day we found "buff," so-called, provided for our meals at the various stations on the road. We found no reason to complain of it; although not so very tender, it was, at all events, preferable to Texas beef.

The buffalo herds, as is generally known, follow the grass; in the spring of the year they travel from south to north, in the fall they retreat from north to south. When railway trains first crossed the prairie, interrupting the march, in single file, of the advancing buffaloes, they would gallop alongside the track for miles, endeavouring to get north or south by heading off the train, instead of waiting for the cars to pass them.

The several lines of railway in this section of the country are spoken of as the U. P., C. P., D. P., K. P.; M. P., referring to the Union, the Central, the Denver, the Kansas, or the Missouri Pacific.

It seemed to be a pretty general opinion that the route of the Union Pacific had been carelessly planned, and already two other lines are projected to shorten the distance, and to pass through a more fertile country; probably through Colorado, by way of Denver, to San Francisco.

Towards evening we again entered the cultivated lands of Kansas, and, travelling all night, we arrived early on Saturday, the 6th, at Kansas City, on the banks of the Missouri, and felt ourselves to be once again in the civilized world.

Kansas City has the present reputation of being the hardest, roughest place in the West; we at least had no opportunity to form an opinion, for we left again immediately, and, travelling all day through the well-cultivated, fertile State of Missouri, we reached Saint Louis on Saturday night at 9 P.M., having been exactly six days and five nights continuously, in transit from the shores of the Pacific to the banks of the Mississippi. We found excellent quarters at the Southern Hotel, and very much enjoyed the change from portable, to fixed and comfortable beds.

SAINT LOUIS.

We spent a quiet pleasant Sunday on the banks of the Mississippi, the Father of Waters. We attended service at the Episcopal Church, and in the afternoon visited the park and the gardens of Mr. Shaw, laid out and well-maintained in the English style, as the people of the city are very proud to tell you.

This city, favoured by nature and the providence of passing events, contains more than 300,000 inhabitants, and from the great advantages of water-carriage which it possesses, its central situation, and the fertile character of the surrounding country, it seems almost certain, that Saint Louis will eventually become the largest and most important city of the West, if it does not out-rival New York itself.

The immense deposit of iron known as the Iron Mountain, or Pilate Knob, distant only eighty miles from the city, converted by coal now discovered in the immediate vicinity, must eventually enable Saint Louis to undersell Pittsburgh, and to control the iron trade of the Western and Pacific States.

The streets of Saint Louis are well-built and handsome, and we noticed here a more settled appearance of things than in Chicago. An iron bridge, on stone piers, is at present in course of construction across the Mississippi, and it is expected when completed, in a year or eighteen months hence, to add very materially to the trade and importance of the place.

We visited the Fair Grounds, where a meeting, similar to our agricultural associations, takes place yearly. The Rotunda, which is covered in, with sloping seats, is said to accommodate 40,000 people, and to have been filled last autumn. In the centre, on a broad, well-watered ring, trotting horses and prize stock are exhibited and judged; the grounds contain ample and permanent sheds and pens. Probably for size and convenience, the arrangements are unequalled either in or out of the States. The prizes, the result of subscription, are both numerous and valuable; we were informed that the premium for the best cotton was this season fixed at 2000*l*. We should have liked to have remained here longer, but being obliged to push on, at 8 P.M. we crossed the Mississippi in a coach on board a steam-ferry, and at eleven the same evening we arrived at Springfield, in Illinois.

SPRINGFIELD.

SPRINGFIELD, the capital and seat of Government for the State of Illinois, gave us a very good idea of an American country town.

The streets are wide, and rather overgrown with grass, planted on both sides with well-grown healthy-looking trees. In the streets beyond the business part of the town, we found snug and handsome villas, surrounded by gardens, lawns and shrubberies; everything was green and fresh; an air of home and of comfort seemed to prevail at Springfield.

The new State House in course of construction is estimated to cost eight millions of dollars, and will, when completed, be the finest on the Continent.

In the Oakwood Cemetery, which is beautifully laid out, are the remains of President Lincoln (a native of the town), and a monument 100 feet in height, of granite brought from Massachusetts, is being erected of immense proportions, the cost being defrayed by subscription, from all the States of the Union.

Springfield is an enterprising and important little town, possessing good hotels, and several wealthy and well-managed banks: there is coal in the immediate neighbourhood (and indeed all through the State). They have elevators and woollen mills, and a very large watch manufactory is in course of construction, at which we found them manufacturing, without assistance, the very intricate and delicate machinery necessary for this trade.

NIAGARA.

We left Springfield at twelve P.M. on Tuesday, the ninth of April, and passing through Chicago at half-past seven on the following day, we arrived the same evening at Detroit, on the Canadian frontier, and travelling through Canada during the night, we arrived at four the next morning at Niagara Falls.

We have no intention of attempting to picture this wonder of the world, so often and so well described. But description can never convey to the mind, the least idea of that immense and never-ceasing fall of waters, passing day and night to the ocean, dating from ages beyond the records of man, and pouring, as it will doubtless still pour, till the end of time itself.

The following day we travelled by rail, in a drawing-room car, down the beautiful banks of the Hudson River, and through the busy, pleasant towns which are to be found on its banks, past the handsome country-seats and parks of well-to-do New York citizens. Surrounded by rocks, rivers, and mountains, on heavy-timbered, good grass land, these country-seats seemed to possess every advantage which nature can supply.

About noon the same day, Friday, the twelfth, we reached New York, having completed our return journey from Ocean to Ocean.

SLEEPING CARS.

If Christopher Columbus was the discoverer of America, Lincoln the emancipator of the coloured men, Washington the father of his country, and Grant its greatest general, "Pullman" must have the credit of being one of its greatest benefactors. It would be simply impossible for human nature to travel such immense distances, without the comforts and conveniences which the "Pullman" cars supply.

There are certainly other sleeping cars, but none so good as Pullman's, which are thoroughly well built, handsomely furnished, and fitted with double windows to keep out the dust. These other cars are built of slighter stuff, with single windows, poorly fitted, and given to "telescoping," *i.e.*, to collapse as a telescope with pressure from behind. Sleeping cars are each about 60 feet long by 12 feet across, containing eighteen sofas and eighteen upper berths; thus providing sleeping accommodation for thirty-six persons. The upper berth is let down at night, but is closed during the day, when a stranger would be quite unable to guess at its existence. Being heavy, and well hung on springs, they roll along very comfortably. The wheels are placed together at each end of the long body. Pullman's cars have six at each end; the others run on four.

Each end of the sleeper is "fixed" with stoves for heating the car, lavatory and dressing-room; one for the use of ladies, and the other, of course, for gentlemen. A coloured attendant is attached to each car, neatly dressed in a grey uniform, whose business it is to attend to the beds, to keep the car swept out and in good order, to look after the icewater, and to act as footman for the benefit of his passengers. We found them generally quiet and attentive.

Life in the car begins soon after daylight. Some passengers from habit, others from inclination, prefer to rise early. The movements of those who are stirring, and the immediate subsequent conversation on the subject of dollars, population of the "cities," and value of town lots, close to the curtains, make it quite impossible for anybody to take a little . more sleep, even if there were time, before breakfast, which is arranged very early.

After breakfast, smoking in the rotunda, at the rear of the car, conversation, cards, and reading, fill up the time till dinner, generally about twelve. Smoking and reading occupy the time till supper, about seven, after which the beds are very promptly made up, the curtains are drawn, and the sleeping-car full of sleepers is being whirled along into the wilderness. In making up these beds for the night they prepare them invariably for the feet towards the engine.

The bedding is changed every evening, and the cars swept down twice daily. The only drawbacks we found to be the scramble in the morning for the washing apparatus; and there seemed to be some difficulty about the ladies' hair-dressing, which was sometimes performed rather too publicly.

A boy travels with every train, and passing from car to car, offers for sale apples, oranges, candy, figs, newspapers, books, and sundries. We found it a good plan to turn him into a circulating library by giving him "quarters" for the use of his books; but, generally, there is an indisposition to read, and people move about from seat to seat, and join very generally in conversation with their neighbours.

When choosing your quarters in a sleeper, you will

find it a good plan to select the car in rear of the train, as there is not so much passing backwards and forwards, and less chance of trouble if you run off the track; and if possible, engage your section in the middle of the car, where you can get away from the stoves, which are frequently overheated, and you avoid the rattle of the wheels, to which the end sections are liable. If you engage the entire section you secure yourself against having an early-rising, noisy, or heavy man sleeping in the bed above you, and you have the entire control, by day as well as night, of a carpeted room six feet square, with two sofas, two windows, two spittoons, and a heavy curtain, which is drawn at night, protecting the bed from draughts, and secluding you entirely from public observation.

The sleeping cars, as we understood, are the property of the Pullman Company, and are run by the railway companies, with a view to increase their traffic, free of cost; a separate charge for the use of them being made and collected by the Pullman conductors.

If you leave the car at any time you must be very quick in your movements if you do not care to get left behind on the road. There is no bell-ringing, no porters to open and close the doors. The conductor, shouting, "All on board!" immediately jumps himself on board, and the train moves forward without any further warning.

The cost of these cars ranges from 4000*l*. to 5000*l*. The track, as a rule, we found to be well laid, and maintained in good working order. Over the plains the earth has been simply thrown into the middle from a shallow ditch on each side of the line, upon which heavy sleepers are laid about a foot apart; the rails are then placed upon them, and "there you are." The construction of the Union Pacific averaged a mile daily; and sometimes three miles were made in one day. There is not so much cutting along the entire length of three thousand miles as in the sixty miles from London to Brighton.

The line generally is safe and easy to travel over; and although it is opposed to good manners to abuse the bridge which carried you over, we must say that the wood-work seemed to us rather shaky. There is a great deal of what is termed "trestle-work," particularly between Ogden and San Francisco, about which we came to the same conclusion as a gentleman from California, who "guessed it wasn't any too strong, you bet."

Accidents of a less serious nature than telescoping sometimes occur in the sleeping cars. Two gentlemen, travelling to Washington, joined the train so late one night as to find all but one of the large lower berths engaged, and this they agreed to share; but the snoring and struggling of one partner, obliged the other to dissolve the partnership, and he went off to finish his journey in the conductor's seat at the rear of the car. Presently a middle-aged lady arrives and demands sleeping accommodation. The gentleman who had turned out offers her the use of the space he had previously occupied, saying that his little son was there, but that she was welcome to lie down, if she cared to do so. This was gratefully accepted, and the lady retired to compose herself. Presently the snoring and kicking were renewed. "Lie still and be quiet, sonny," said the lady, patting her neighbour on the back. "Hullo!" exclaimed the sleeper. "What's the matter? I'm not your sonny. I'm a member of the West Virginia Legislature."

On the outward trip, on the day we passed through Cheyenne, there had been an execution, and some very hard-looking men joined the train. It was guessed that they had come down from Montana to amuse themselves; and one of them, having a fancy for our section, quietly occupied it, and taking out a pistol from that dreadful back-pocket, placed it on his knees and began playing with it. Theodore, our coloured boy, explained to him that the seat was previously occupied; but as he guessed it would do very well for him so far as he was going, the conductor was called in, who informed him that the seat would cost him eight dollars if he remained there for ten minutes. He then moved forward, to the general relief of those who were present. We understood that he stepped off " somewhere " during the night; at all events, we were fortunate enough not to see any more of him.

INDIANS.

THERE isn't much fun in an Indian; if there is, it lies deepish down. There certainly wasn't much fun in the specimens of the noble red men that we came across: they are to be found at most of the depôts from the Platte to the Nevada, generally shoeless, covered in red blankets, in an idle sort of way begging "quarters" from passengers, which is immediately exchanged for whiskey, or disposed of by gambling, to which they are passionately addicted. These wretched aborigines, living in huts of the meanest kind, seem very little removed in intellect from the dogs which follow them.

But there are other Indians far away on the plains who still hunt the buffalo, and take scalps from the white man whenever a safe opportunity presents itself. Near Fort Laramie, Cedric was pointed out to us close to the line, where, some eighteen months since, White Cloud surprised and destroyed a large party of troops; and at Cheyenne, an officer joined the train who told us of an expedition he had recently returned from, in which he had disposed of nine out of eleven, pretty much as if he had been speaking of a covey of partridges.

When we were at Denver, there was a rumour that a station on the Kansas Pacific, had been attacked by Indians the previous day, but it turned out that it was simply a trading party who had come in for tobacco.

There are no doubt hostile Indians in the neighbourhood of Kit Carson, but they are busy with the buffaloes at this season of the year, and, moreover, they have a religious dread of attacking the line, for they know too well that the consequences would be fatal, for the Government would avenge it at whatever cost.

There are settlements of peaceable Indians in Minnesota, who live on lands reserved to them by the State, and on food provided at the public expense; but, so far as we could learn, they are idle and worthless, averse to all labour. The brick houses provided for them, they make use of to stable their ponies, preferring themselves to live in their miserable wooden huts or in tents.

We are unwilling to close this diary without again expressing our sincere thanks to the friends we have left behind us; nothing can exceed their hospitality and kindness. Outside of the newspapers we have nowhere seen or even heard of the Fenians; we have nowhere found anything but kind and friendly feeling towards England.

We found nothing of the resentment so frequently and erroneously stated to exist here, against all pretensions to rank, title, or wealth. In dress the ladies aim to "head off" Paris itself; the fashions for gentlemen's apparel in New York are closely following those of London; footmen, cockades and livery are to be seen in all the larger cities.

Self-appointed colonels, honourables, squires, and judges abound in the Western States; lodges, parks, glass, and well-arranged grounds are to be found attached to most of the best country-seats; and dining in West Nineteenth Street, or elsewhere, *à la Russe,* you find in the *menu* everything which London or Paris can supply.

Game, and even the canvas-backed ducks are preserved; pheasants are being imported from England, and quail are being brought from Illinois to the State of New York.

Game laws are in force all over the Union, and in some instances are more severe than in England. It would thus appear that America does not, as is generally supposed, oppose herself to the well-settled customs of the Old World, but rather, as population and wealth increases, that we shall find her more and more generally adapting herself to those customs, invariably associated with the enjoyment of luxury, and the possession of wealth.

We claim forbearance from criticism, for our journal has been written entirely from memory on the return voyage, without the assistance of notes or books of reference.

The stranger about to travel, as we did, for information and pleasure will find an intelligent, kind-hearted population, and the country everything which we have endeavoured to describe.

The intending settler will find abundance of land, and a choice of climates, awaiting him, and almost certain prosperity, if he has the head and the heart to persevere; but one thing is very certain—he must not wait for assistance from "Jupiter." When every one is keen and busy about you, it will not answer to be "fooling around." To succeed in the United States of America, a man must either "fish or cut bait."

On Wednesday, the 17th May, at 3 P.M., we went on board the Guion steamship "Wisconsin," Capt. Williams, bound for Liverpool, and, as on the "Colorado," we found excellent quarters, an abundant table, and attention and kindness from every one. About twelve hundred miles from New York, off the banks, almost in mid-ocean, in a dense lifting fog, we came across the barque "Columbus," bound with China clay from Falmouth to Boston; a collision occurred carrying away her figure-head and bowsprit, which in passing cut through our rigging, smashing the bulwarks and iron stanchions of the quarter-deck boats, much as a sickle cuts through grain. Nothing but the promptness and skill with which the steamer was handled, prevented our sending the barque and the China clay, to trade with the mermaids at the bottom of the ocean, where we might very possibly have been compelled to follow her.

We completed an unusually smooth and pleasant voyage of twelve days, in which we doubt if anybody even "suffered from the sea," by landing at Queenstown on Sunday afternoon, the 28th of May.

MARCH, 1871.

March 1.
,, 2.
,, 3.
,, 4.
,, 5.
,, 6.
,, 7.
,, 8.
,, 9.
,, 10.
,, 11.
,, 12.
,, 13.
,, 14.
,, 15. Left Liverpool 3 P.M.
,, 16. Queenstown 2 P.M.
,, 17. Ran 189 miles.
,, 18. ,, 246 ,,
,, 19. ,, 260 ,,
,, 20. ,, 208 ,,
,, 21. ,, 188 ,,
,, 22. ,, 242 ,,
,, 23. ,, 231 ,,
,, 24. ,, 160 ,,
,, 25. ,, 219 ,,
,, 26. ,, 182 ,,
,, 27. ,, 165 ,,
,, 28. ,, 198 ,,
,, 29. ,, 247 ,,
,, 30. ,, 135 ,,
Landed 12 A.M.
,, 31. New York.

APRIL.

April 1. New York.
,, 2. ,,
,, 3. ,,
,, 4. ,,
,, 5. ,,
,, 6. Boston.
,, 7. ,,
,, 8. ,,
,, 9. Easter Sunday.
,, 10. Left for Philadelphia.
,, 11. Philadelphia.
,, 12. Washington.
,, 13. Baltimore.
,, 14. ,,
,, 15. Pittsburgh.
,, 16. Cincinnati.
,, 17. ,,
,, 18. Chicago.
,, 19. Crossed Mississippi.
,, 20. Crossed Missouri.
,, 21. On the Plains.
,, 22. Arrived at Ogden.
,, 23. Salt Lake.
,, 24. ,, ,,
,, 25. On the Plains.
,, 26. Crossed the Nevadas.
,, 27. San Francisco.
,, 28. ,, ,,
,, 29. ,, ,,
,, 30. Santa Clara.

MAY.

May 1. Left San Francisco, 8 A.M.
„ 2. Nevadas.
„ 3. Plains.
„ 4. Denver.
„ 5. Buffalo.
„ 6. Kansas City to St. Louis.
„ 7. St. Louis.
„ 8. „
„ 9. Springfield.
„ 10. Chicago.
„ 11. Niagara.
„ 12. Albany and Hudson.
„ 13. Philadelphia.
„ 14. New York.

May 15. New York
„ 16. „
„ 17. Left ditto at 3 P.M.
„ 18. Ran 196 miles.
„ 19. „ 256 „
„ 20. „ 244 „
„ 21. „ 254 „
„ 22. „ 252 „
„ 23. „ 257 „
„ 24. „ 268 „
„ 25. „ 264 „
„ 26. „ 280 „
„ 27. „ 266 „
„ 28. Queenstown 3 P.M.
„ 29.
„ 30.
„ 31.

APPENDIX.

APPENDIX.

GREAT CALIFORNIA LINE.
Condensed Time Table.

On and after May 22nd, 1870, Trains leave Chicago from Wells Street Depôt, as follows:—

STATIONS.	PACIFIC EX. Except Sundays. Through Connection.	EXPRESS MAIL. Except Saturdays.	Distance from Chicago.
LEAVE.			Miles.
CHICAGO	10.30 A.M.	9.15 P.M.	....
Dixon	2.20 P.M.	1.33 A.M.	98
Sterling	2.45 ,,	2.05 ,,	110
Fulton	3.45 ,,	3.10 ,,	136
Clinton	4.00 ,,	3.25 ,,	138
Cedar Rapids	7.40 ,,	7.35 ,,	219
Boone	1.15 A.M.	1.40 P.M.	341
Grand Junction	2.45 ,,	3.22 ,,	363
Missouri Valley Junction	7.20 ,,	8.41 ,,	467
ARRIVE.			
COUNCIL BLUFFS	8.20 ,,	9.50 ,,	488
OMAHA	9.00 ,,	10.20 ,,	492
LEAVE—OMAHA TIME.		Elevation.	
OMAHA	11.00 ,,	966 feet.	....
Cheyenne	11.50 ,,	6,041 ,,	1,009
Bryan	6.30 ,,	6,340 ,,	1,359
Ogden	6.00 P.M.	4,340 ,,	1,533
Corinne	6.45 ,,	4,294 ,,	1,550
Elko	9.00 A.M.	5,030 ,,	1,799
Argenta	1.05 P.M.	4,575 ,,	1,871
Reno	2.10 A.M.	4,525 ,,	2,113
Sacramento	1.10 P.M.	56 ,,	2,267
Stockton	3.25 ,,	46 ,,	2,315
San Francisco	7.00 ,,	....	2,391

First Class Hotels and Eating Houses at Convenient Points along the Line.

20 Miles the Shortest Route to Moline, Rock Island and Davenport, and no change of Cars, *viâ* C. and N. W. Railway. Trains leave at 10.30 A.M. and 9.15 P.M.

GRAND
VOCAL & INSTRUMENTAL CONCERT
ON BOARD THE S.S. "COLORADO,"
WEDNESDAY, MARCH 29, 1871.

Patron	CAPTAIN FREEMAN.
President	HENRY NASH, Esq.
Treasurer	P. W. FLOWER, Esq.
Master of Ceremonies	DR. LATHAM.
Director of Festival	R. CHRISTMAS, Esq.

PROGRAMME.

OVERTURE—BRASS BAND.   FANTASIA—CHRISTY'S MINSTRELS.

Song	Mr. MORRISON.	
Trombone Solo	Mr. PRIESTLY	The Death of Wellington.
Song	Mr. ROBINSON	We yet may meet again.
Song	Mr. CHADWICK	Friar of Orders Grey.
Cornet Solo	Mr. BENT	Torquato Tasso.
Song	Capt. FREEMAN	Sparking Sunday Night.
Song	Mr. RICHARDSON.	
String Band		Waltz.
Song	Mr. MARSDEN	Bonnie Bessie Grey.
Song	Mr. FLOWER	Rosa Lee, the Prairie Flower.
String Band		Galop.
Song	Mr. ROWE	The Wolf.
String Band		Hail Columbia and Dixies Land.
Song	Mr. CHADWICK	Scots wha hae wi' Wallace Bled.
Cornet and Bombardon Obligato		Messrs. EMIDY & McMAHON.

FINALE.
GOD SAVE THE QUEEN.

Commencing at 7.30 precisely.

BILL OF FARE.
Steam Ship "Colorado," 17th day of March, 1871.

DINNER.

Soups.—Fish, Chouder, and Pea.	Roast Goose and Apple Sauce.
Fish.—Turbot and Soles, Anchovy and Parsley Sauce.	Roast and Boiled Fowls.
	Harricot Ox Tail.
Roast Beef and Roast Potatoes.	Pork Cutlets.
Boiled Mutton and Caper Sauce.	Corned Beef and Cabbage.

PASTRY.

Blackcap Pudding.	Prunes and Custard.
Corn Flour Pudding.	Lemon Cheese Cakes.
Rhubarb Pies.	Marmalade Open Tart.

APPENDIX. 79

KANSAS CITY.

THE CITY OFFICIALS, COMPLETE.

THE city government, by yesterday's swearing in of the new policemen, is now complete. For convenience we give the names of the officers:—

CITY GOVERNMENT.

Mayor—Wm. Warner.
Auditor—Jno. J. Tobin.
Treasurer—Samuel Jarboe.
Attorney—J. W. Dunlap.
Recorder—D. A. N. Grover.
Marshal—Thos. M. Speers.
Superintendent of Registration—R. M. Roth.
Collector—P. M. Chouteau.
Assessor—R. Salisbury.
Engineer—O. Chanute.
Physician—W. C. Evans.
Clerk—Dan. Geary.
Market Master—R. C. Gould.
Wharf Master—A. T. Hoover.
Superintendent of Fire Department—Jas. McMennamin.
Inspector of Weights and Measures—Wm. Tobener.

COMMON COUNCIL.

First Ward—Junius Chaffee, John Campbell, Wm. Weston.
Second Ward—J. W. Keefer, Philip Henn, H. T. Hovelman.
Third Ward—Jonas Lykins, D. Ellison, Joab Toney.
Fourth Ward—J. E. Marsh, James Hannon, Thos. Burke.

POLICEMEN.

Sergeants—E. Gillooly and J. P. Fayman.
Privates—Michael Halpine, Patrick Brady, John Murphy, H. R. Kelso, Oliver Allen, Thomas Fitzpatrick, Tillman Crabtree, Peter T. Rivard, Miles Bulger, James McKnight, Charles Dripps, Con. O'Hare, Michael Maloney, Thomas Cavanagh, M. Mahoney, Jas. Bradley, John Galligher, Patrick Green, John C. Bescher, Peter Engle, Geo. E. Miles, E. H. Russell, John P. Westberg.

GRAND HOTEL,
SAN FRANCISCO, CALIFORNIA.

JOHNSON & CO. - - - - Proprietors.

Breakfast, from 6 to 11. Lunch, from 12½ to 2½.
Dinner, from 5½ to 7½. Supper, from 9 to 11.
Breakfast on Sundays at 8 o'clock. Children's Dinner at 5.

BREAKFAST.

Coffee. Green Tea. Black Tea. Japan Tea. Chocolate.

FISH.
Broiled Fresh Salmon. Smoked Salmon. Salt Mackerel. Smelt.

BROILED.
Beef Steaks. Sirloin Steaks. Mutton Chops. Veal Chops. Pork Chops.
Veal Cutlets. Bacon. Black Pudding. Liver. Ham.

FRIED, ETC.
Veal Cutlets breaded. Bacon and Liver. Kidney. Tripe. Ham and Eggs.
Pork. House Sausages. Sausage Balls. Codfish Balls.
Smoked Beef. Meat Hash. Stewed Tripe.

COLD.
Roast Beef. Mutton. Ham. Corned Beef.

EGGS.
Boiled. Fried. Scrambled. Poached, on Toast.
Omelettes, plain, or with Parsley, Onions, Ham, Kidney, Cheese, or Spanish style.

POTATOES.
Baked. Fried. Stewed. A la Lyonnaise.

BREAD, ETC.
Domestic Bread. French Bread. Boston Brown Bread. Graham Bread.
Corn Bread. Hot Rolls.
English Muffins. Egg Muffins. Waffles. Batter Cakes. Buckwheat Cakes.
Corn Mush, fried. Dry and Dipped Toast. Boiled Hominy.
Boiled Mush. Cracked Wheat.

Children occupying Seats at the Public Table will be charged full price.
All meals sent to rooms will invariably be charged extra.
Persons leaving word at the Office can have meals served at any hour.
AFTER HALF-PAST TEN O'CLOCK, BREAKFAST WILL BE SERVED IN THE CLUB ROOM.

GRAND HOTEL.
WINE LIST.

CHAMPAGNE.
	Drs. c.
Louis Rœderer Carte Blanche	4 00
„ „ „ „ pts.	2 00
Veuve Cliquot Ponsardin	4 00
„ „ „ pts.	2 00
Sparkling Moselle, "Kupferberg"	3 00
Krug (private cuvée), qts.	4 00
„ „ „ pts.	2 00
Carte Blanche Ruinart, Père & Fils	4 00
„ „ „ pts.	2 00
Chas. Heidsieck	3 00
Carte D'Or	4 00
Lac D'Or	3 00
Schrieder	3 50

CLARET.
Grand Vin de Chateau Lafitte, (Tenet & De George)	3 00
Grau, La Rose, Bert & Co.	2 00
Chateau de Frands	1 50
Our Own	1 00
Lognac	1 50
Chateau Leoville	1 50
Medoc	1 00
St. Loubes	1 00

HAUT SAUTERNE.
Cantegrit	3 50
Chateau Yquem, Dubois & Co.	3 00
Pondesac, Vergez	1 50

HOCK.
Steinberger Cabinet	3 00
Liebfraumilch	1 50
Hockheimer	1 50

BURGUNDY.
Chambertin, Ermitage	4 00
Chablis	2 50

MADEIRA.
Fine Old Extra	4 00
London Dock	4 00

PORT.
Offley's	3 00
Fine Old Dry	2 50

SHERRY.
Harmony	2 50
Old Amontillado	3 00
Table Sherry	1 50

CALIFORNIA WINES.
	Drs. c.
Private Cuvée, Landsberger's	1 50
Sparkling California Muscatel, Landsberger's	1 50
Do, pints	1 00
Pearl Hock (Woods'), very fine vintage 1861	1 50
Port, qts.	1 00
White Wine „	0 75
Angelica „	0 75
Cucomongo	0 75
„ Madeira	1 00
Lake Vineyard Claret	0 50
Mound Vineyard	0 75
Sultana	0 75
Quiquiriqui Red Wine	0 75
Chambertin	1 00
Sparkling Catawba, Cincinnati	2 00

BRANDY.
Serris, Père & Fils, 1835	5 00
Martell	3 00
S. O. P.	2 50
Otard, Dupuy & Co.	2 50

WHISKIES.
Cabinet	1 50
Bourbon	1 00
Rye	1 50
Scotch Whisky, Islay	1 50
St. Croix Rum	1 50
Jamaica Rum	1 50

ENGLISH ALE AND PORTER.
Tennent's Ale, qts.	0 75
„ „ pts.	0 50
Morice, Cox & Co., pts.	0 50
Guinness' Dublin Stout, qts.	0 75
„ „ „ pts.	0 50
Wintringham's Crab-apple Cider	1 00

LIQUEURS.
Annisette	Carmeline
Maraschino	Chartreuse
Kirschwasser	Absynthe
Curaçoa, red	Curaçoa, white
Pousse Café	Cherry Cordial

Saratoga, Seltzer, Vichy, Pacific Congress, and Napa Soda Waters.

CORKAGE, 50 CENTS PER BOTTLE.

G

GRAND HOTEL DINNER.

San Francisco, Saturday, April 29, 1871.

SOUP.
Green Turtle.   Split Pea.

FISH.
Boiled Salmon, Egg Sauce.   Boiled Sturgeon, Tomato Sauce.
Fried Smelts.

COLD.
Soused Pig's Feet.
Corned Beef.   Ham.   Tongue.   Mutton.

BOILED.
Corned Pork.   Leg of Mutton, Caper Sauce.   Bacon.
Corned Beef and Cabbage.

ENTRÉES.
Riz de Veau, Sauce Tomato.
    Calf's Liver, Larded with Mushrooms.
        Bird Pie.
            Baked Pork and Beans.
                Giblet Saute, Aux Champignons.
                    Fricaseed Tripe.
                        Sheep's Feet, Sauce Piquante.

ROAST.
Pig, Apple Sauce.
Loin of Mutton.   Spring Lamb, Mint Sauce.   Beef.
    Ham, Champagne Sauce.   Shoulder of Mutton, stuffed.
Pork.   Veal Stuffed.   Mutton.

RELISHES.
Stewed Rhubarb.
Horse Radish.   Assorted Pickles.   Peppers.
    Cranberries.   Beets.   Olives.

VEGETABLES.
Onions.   Asparagus.   Mashed Turnips.
    New Potatoes.   Stewed Tomatoes.   Hominy.
        Mashed Potatoes.   Boiled Rice.

PASTRY.
Gooseberry Pie.   Currant Pudding, Brandy Sauce.   Rhubarb Pie.

DESSERT.
Almonds.   Walnuts.   Apples.   Assorted Cakes.
    Oranges.   Strawberry Ice-cream.

TEA AND COFFEE.

APPENDIX.

Continental Hotel,
PHILADELPHIA.

J. E. KINGSLEY & CO.	PROPRIETORS.

Dinner:
TUESDAY, APRIL 11th, 1871.

SOUP.
Gumbo.	Barley.

FISH.
Baked Cod, Genevoise Sauce.	Boiled Halibut, Hollandaise Sauce.

BOILED.
Corned Beef and Cabbage.	Jole.	Boiled Turkey, Oyster Sauce.
Leg Mutton, Caper Sauce.	Capons and Pork, Egg Sauce.

COLD DISHES.
Boned Turkey.	Corned Beef.
Chicken.	Chicken Salad.	Lobster.	Ham.

ENTREES.
Blanquettes of Veal, with Green Peas.	Calves' Tongues, a l'Italian.
Mutton Cutlets, breaded, Madeira Sauce.	Macaroni, with Cream.
Rissole of Chicken, a la Parisian.	Broiled Ducks, a la Diable.
Escalopes of Pork, a la Robert.

ROAST.
Beef.	Leg Mutton.	Turkey.	Chicken.
Ham, Champagne Sauce.	Lamb, Mint Sauce.

RELISHES.
Worcestershire Sauce.	Stuffed Mangoes.
Lettuce.	Horse Radish.	Gherkins.
Chow Chow.	Cranberry Sauce.	Cole-slaw.	French Mustard.
Queen Olives.	Radishes.

VEGETABLES.
Mashed Potatoes.	Beets, pickled or plain.	Boiled Rice.
Boiled Potatoes.	Boiled Hominy.	Corn.
Boiled Sweet Potatoes.	Onions.	Cabbage.
Baked Sweet Potatoes.	Spinach.	Stewed Tomatoes.
Yellow Turnips.	White Turnips.

PASTRY.
Frozen Custard.
Apple Pie.	Mince Pie.	Cream Pie.
Meringue, Vanilla Sauce.	Currant Cake.	Confectionery.

DESSERT.
Raisins.	Coffee and Tea.	Pecans.
Almonds.	Oranges.	Filberts.
English Walnuts.	Apples.	Crackers and Cheese.
Orange Water Ice.

CONTINENTAL HOTEL.

WINE LIST.

CHAMPAGNE.

G. H. Mumm & Co.'s Verzenay	$3 50
G. H. Mumm & Co.'s Verzenay, dry	3 50
G. H. Mumm & Co.'s Extra Dry	4 00
G. H. Mumm & Co., Carte Blanche	4 50
Schreider Anchor	4 00
Schreider, Dry	4 00
Heidsieck & Co., Dry Monopole	4 00
Heidsieck, Piper & Co.	3 50
Heidsieck & Co.	3 00
De Venoge & Co., Carte Blanche	3 00
Bruch, Foucher & Co.'s Carte d'Or.	3 50
Giesler & Co.'s Dry Sillery	3 50
Giesler & Co.'s Gold Label	4 00
Moet & Chandon's Verzenay	4 00
Moet & Chandon's Imperial Green Seal	4 50
Veuve Clicquot, Ponsardin	4 50
L. Roederer's Imperial	4 00
Roderer's Dry Sillery	4 00
Roderer's Carte Blanche	4 50
St. Marceaux	3 50
PINTS OF THE ABOVE, $2.00 TO $2.50.	

CLARET.

Impt. by P. Stevens, from Cruse & Fil, Frères.

Table . . . . . pts. 50; qts.	$1 00
St. Julien	1 50
St. Julien, 1st quality	2 00
Chateau La Rose	3 00
Chateau La Rose, 1st quality	3 50
Chateau Leoville	3 00
Chateau Leoville, 1st quality	3 50
Chateau Latour	4 00
Pomy's d'Estournel	4 00
Chateau Lafitte	5 00
Chateau Margaux	4 00
PINTS OF THE ABOVE, $1.00 TO $2.75.	
Pontet Canet	4 00
Grand Vin du Chateau Rauzan, 1858	5 00
Chateau Lafitte, 1851	5 00
Chateau Margaux, 1851	5 00
Grand Vin, Chateau Leoville	5 00
Grand Vin, Chateau Lafitte	6 00
Chateau Margaux, 1847	7 00
Chateau Lafitte de Monopole, 1847	7 00
Chateau Lafitte Grand Vin, 1841	7 00
Grand Vin de Monopole	8 00

CLARET.

From Barton & Guestier.

Leoville, 1851	$5
Chateau La Rose, 1851	5
La Rose, 1844	6
Chateau Lafitte, 1844	7

BURGUNDY.

Pomard	$4
Sparkling St. Peray	4
Nuits	5
Chambertin	5
Romanee Conti	6
Clos Vougeot, best in the world	7
PINTS OF THE ABOVE, $2.25 TO $3.75.	

SAUTERNE.

From Cruse & Fil, Frères.

Sauterne	$1
Haut Sauterne	2
Count Saluce	4
Latour Blanche, sweet	3
Chablis	4
PINTS OF THE ABOVE, $0.75 TO $2.50.	
Chateau Yquem . pts. $2.75; qts.	5
Johnson & Son's	3

BRANDIES.

Imported by P. Stevens.

Jas. Hennessy & Co., 1846, pale and dark	$5
Jas. Hennessy & Co., 1836, pale	6
Otard, Dupuy & Co., 1846, pale and dark	5
Otard, Dupuy & Co., pale	3
Otard, Dupuy & Co., 1836, pale	5
Otard, Dupuy & Co., 1820, pale	6
Otard, Dupuy & Co., 1800, pale	7
United Vineyard Prop.'s Cognac Vintage, '36	5
United Vineyard Prop.'s Cognac Vintage, '46	4

PORT.

Sandeman's . pts. $1.50; qts.	$2
White Port, very old, Warre Bros.	4
Old Port, from selected grapes	4

ITALIAN WINES.

Lachryma Christi	$2
Capri	2

APPENDIX.

WINE LIST—*continued.*

MADEIRA.

Monterio . . . pts. $1.50 ; qts.	$2 50
Leacock's Old London Particular .	4 00
Don Pedro, reserved stock . . .	4 00
Victoria	4 00
Emperor of Russia	5 00
Revere, Vintage 1825 . . .	5 00
Georgia, very old, high flavoured .	5 50
Carolina	5 50
Sir John Keene	6 50
South Side, old and delicate. . .	6 00
Old Virginia	6 50
N. & M. £100, 1818	10 00
Monterio's Meteor, J. W. Boott. .	6 50
Welsh's Old Family	8 00
Curious Old Pale, selected fr. Maris' gift wine	10 00
Dr. Haro's Old Pale, imported into Philadelphia, 1817	12 00
White Top, T. P. Davis . . .	8 00
Israel Thorndike's Sercial . . .	14 00
Gibb's Old Pale, Newport, 40 years old	15 00

HOCK.

Imp. by P. Stevens from D. Leiden, Cologne

Niersteiner	$2 50
Deidesheimer	3 00
Hockheimer	3 50
Marcobrunner, delicate . . .	5 00
Sparkling Johannisberg, Nonpareil.	4 50
Sparkling Hock	4 00
Red Seal	6 00
Leibfraumilch	4 00

PINTS OF THE ABOVE, $1.50 TO $3.25.

Yellow Seal, pts.$2.75; qts. ⎫	5 00
Green Seal, 1846 . . . ⎪ Johannisberg, from Prince Metternich's Cabinet.	8 00
Silver Bronze Seal, 1846 . ⎬	10 50
Gold Bronze Seal, 1842 . ⎭	12 00
Steinberger, 1846	5 00
Steinberger, Cabinet	8 50

MOSELLE.

Brauneberger, still	$3 00
Scharzberger, still	4 50
Scharzberger, sparkling . . .	5 00
Sparkling Muscatel, Henkell . . pts. $2.25; qts.	4 00
Ausbruch, still and dry . . .	5 00

MOSELLE.

Impt. by Kingsley & Co., from D. Leiden, Cologne.

Scharzberger, Muscatel still pts. $2.50; qts.	$4 50
Sparkling Scharzberger Muscatel .	5 00
Sparkling Moselle Muscatel pts. $2.50 ; qts.	4 50

AMERICAN WINES.

Longworth's Golden Wedding . .	$3 00
Werk's Sparkling Catawba . . .	2 50
California Hock, still.	1 50

PINTS OF THE ABOVE, $1.00 TO $1.75.

Catawba Dry Still	1 50
Unfermented Catawba	2 00
California Port	2 00
Carlifornia Angelica, sweet . . .	2 00

SHERRY.

Three Grapes, full flavour . . .	$2 00
Table, Pale & Brown . pts. $1.25 ; qts.	2 50
Vin de Pasto, extremely delicate .	3 00
Y. Pale, D. Yriartes	3 00
Yriartes' Gold, 1825	3 50
Gastelus' Amontillado	3 50
Mateos & Brother's Sherry, very pale	3 00
Mateos & Brother's Amontillado .	3 50
Cabinet Amontillado	4 00
Queen's	4 00
Gastelus' Old Pale, rich but delicate	3 50
Duartes' V. V. S. Dry Wine . . .	5 00
Hidalgo, Brown	5 00
Revere Cabinet, 1810	4 50
Stevens' Sherry, old and soft. . .	5 50
Prince Albert, pale and free from sweetness	4 50
Stevens' Imperial Vintage, 1840 .	5 50
Imperial Amontillado.	5 00
Competitor, pale, delicate, and pleasing	5 00
Star and Gurter, dry and delicate, from Xeres	5 00
M. L. Emperor Russia	6 00

ALE AND PORTER.

Muir's Ale	$ 50
Burton Ale	50
Bass Ale	50
Barclay & Co., London Porter, pints	50
Dublin Porter, pints	50
American Ale, pints	30
Champagne Cider, pints, 50 ; quarts,	1 00

LIQUORS, CORDIALS, &c.—Le Grand Chartreuse, Curaçoa, Maraschino, Anisette, Kirschwasser, &c. Empire, American and German Mineral Waters.

CORKAGE, $1.00 per bottle. Each waiter is provided with Wine Cards and Pencil.

SALT LAKE THEATRE!

LAST NIGHT

OF THE

Great French Artiste, Mlle. Marietta

RAVEL!

THE UNRIVALLED DANSEUSE, PANTOMIMIST, AND TIGHT ROPE PERFORMER.

SUPPORTED BY THE FAVORITE ACTOR,

GEO. B. WALDRON.

WILL BE PRESENTED THE NEW ORIGINAL DRAMA, BY

CHARLES FOSTER, ESQ.,

OF NEW YORK, ENTITLED,

WILD CAT;

OR, THE

MARRIAGE BY MOONLIGHT.

TO CONCLUDE WITH THE

DUMB GIRL OF GENOA!

APPENDIX. 87

WILL BE PRESENTED THE NEW ORIGINAL DRAMA, BY

CHARLES FOSTER, ESQ.,
OF NEW YORK, ENTITLED,

WILD CAT;
OR, THE

MARRIAGE BY MOONLIGHT.

Florence Elwood,   ..   **MARIETTA RAVEL.**
Known as the Wild Cat
Wm. Elwood, *assuming the name of Jack Rainer*   ..   **Mr. G. B. WALDRON.**

Mr. Elwood, *a Broker*	Mr. A. THORNE.
Frederick Verney	Mr. D. J. MCINTOSH.
Bob Stanley, *alias* Mr. Minton	Mr. W. H. POWER.
The Major	Mr. P. MARGETTS.
Peter Perkins	Mr. J. C. GRAHAM.
Mike Mulligan	Mr. W. T. HARRIS.
Jean de Favern, *an old pile driver*	Mr. M. FORSTER.
Deck Hand	Mr. W. CALTON.
Servant	Mr. R. MATTHEWS.
Minister	Mr. H. HORSLEY.
Police Officer	Mr. A. MANN.
Meg Macaloy	Miss A. ADAMS.
Emily Wilton	Mrs. A. CLAWSON.
Mrs. Ashworth	Mrs. M. G. CLAWSON.

To Conclude with the Thrilling Melodrama in one Act, entitled, THE

Dumb Girl of Genoa!

Julietta   ..   ..   **MARIETTA RAVEL.**
Antonio   ..   ..   ..   **Mr. G. B. WALDRON.**

Count Arvenio	Mr. W. H. POWER.
Justin	Mr. M. FORSTER.
Moco	Mr. P. MARGETTS.
Strapado	Mr. J. C. GRAHAM.
Desperatta	Mr. A. THORNE.
Jaspero	Mr. H. HORSLEY.
Whiskeriskis	Mr. J. E. EVANS.

OPERA GLASSES FOR HIRE IN FIRST CIRCLE.

WISCONSIN HALL,
ATLANTIC CITY.

WISCONSIN MINSTRELS' PROGRAMME.

Overture	COMPANY.
"Massa was a Stingy Man"	C. M. COLLINS.
"Blue-eyed Nelly"	T. ASPANALL.
"Down the River"	L. T. MITCHELL.
"Write me a Letter from Home"	J. M'DONALD.
"The Rhine Wine"	P. OLSEN.
"Hallelujah Band"	G. CORBETT.

INTERVAL.

"Good old Jeff and Drapers' Clerk"	C. M. COLLINS.
"Waste not, Want not"	T. ASPANALL.
Comic Sketch,	L. T. MITCHELL.
"Wanted an Orator"	C. M. COLLINS.
"The Sewing Machine," and "Sailors' Alphabet"	G. CORBETT.
"Champagne Charlie"	J. M'DONALD.
"Fifty Years Ago"	P. OLSEN.

FINALE—"GOD SAVE THE QUEEN."

EXTRACT *from* 'THE STAGE,' *Journal of the Drama, Music, &c.*
New York, Saturday, April 8, 1871.

FASHIONABLE GOSSIP.

Miss Fannie Gulbrandsen, of Piermont, N. Y., formerly of Brooklyn, who made her first appearance in society this winter, is a most charming young lady of sweet sixteen summers, and a general favourite in select society.

Mr. John M. Clark, of Piermont, N. Y., will shortly lead to the altar the lovely and accomplished Miss Tillie Gulbrandsen, formerly of Brooklyn.

John W. Farmer, son of the late wealthy philanthropist, is engaged to a charming blonde of Worcester, Mass.

Women are taking a foremost rank as artists. A ladies' Palette Club would be more seasonably sensible than Sorosis.

The annual spring-tide festival of Mr. Jerome Hopkins' Free Orpheonist Choir Schools is announced to take place at the Academy of Music, on the 25th of April. Many fashionable ladies have identified themselves with these concerts.

Mr. and Mrs. W. T. Elliott, of 125th Street, Harlem, celebrated their tin wedding on the evening of March 21st. The evening was agreeably spent by all the guests present.

Young ladies all read evening 'papers now—the gossip particularly.

Several very high-toned wedding ceremonies are announced to culminate after Lent.

Mr. Melville D. Landon, the facile writer and courteous gentleman, resides in Twenty-fourth Street, near the Fifth Avenue Hotel.

Mrs. Ives, an entrancing widow, and daughter of Senator Motley, is engaged to Mr. Vernon Harcourt, a florid and handsome Briton.

Mrs. Paran Stevens, Mrs. Sherwood (a gifted writer), Mrs. General McClellan, Mrs. Barlow, Mrs. Livingston, and Mrs. Sydney Mason, have, through their encouragement, perfected and carried out successfully many social pleasures; the pecuniary result of which went to the benefit of benevolent projects.

"Our Sociable" will give a ball at Delmonico's after Lent.

Miss Appleton, of Twenty-third Street, leaves for Europe during the month.

The Howe-Brownson wedding will come off in June.

We are promised a new style in the arrangement of ladies' hair this spring, something in the Grecian order.

Miss Mav Bevins, of 124th Street, will soon treat her Harlem friends to a series of private theatricals, which promises to be an event of a most recherché character.

Charles R. Brinkerhoff, a son of the celebrated prima donna Madam Clara E. Brinkerhoff, has fallen heir to an estate valued at half a million. Charlie is the lion of the day.

The last meeting of the season of the Ivy Circle will undoubtedly be a grand affair. The sociable will take place at the residence of Mr. John Rutler, foot of East Eighty-fourth Street, on Wednesday evening, April 12th.

The Lyric Club announce their closing on Thursday evening, April 13th, at Lyric Hall. On the following evening, the 14th instant, the Lyric Coterie hold forth at the same place.

Mrs. Livingston's Ball at Delmonico's will inaugurate the short gay after Lenten season.

MASONRY IN THE NEW WORLD.

PART FIRST—DEGREE FIRST.

WOMEN are curious creatures. They are not only so in the eyes of men, but they have a curiosity within themselves which surpasseth all understanding, including their own. I have learned this, and I may as well mention it before going further, for it may do quite as well as a regular preface. At all events, it will explain some things, which is more than prefaces generally do.

I am a quiet man, and I love quiet above all things in the world; but in order to secure it, I have got to take a step that may make my own the fate of Morgan's. I am married. (If I thought my domestic life would be any more peaceful for it, I could at this point a tale unfold, but I withhold, &c.) Little by little my adored Emily Jane has *won* upon me *since* our marriage; that is to say, she has persuaded me that I am slightly her inferior in many respects; that I should listen to and be guided by her in all important questions. As I said before, she has gradually won upon me by keeping continually at it, and now she has got so she *insists* on certain things, and I give up— for the sake of peace.

And yet I do not consider myself a henpecked husband, not by any means. I think I can put a head on any man who dares insinuate that I am. I am a peace man, and rather than have an argument about anything in which she invariably gets the best of it, I have learned to give way with modesty, grace, and dignity.

Before our marriage, I was drifting about loose to some extent, and got into several bad scrapes, the roughest of which was, joining the Masons; thereby hangs a tale. I believe that I mentioned the fact of my wife's gradual *winning* upon me, and however much she was disposed to let me attend lodge during our honeymoon, she soon began to argue with me regarding the propriety of a married man's keeping late hours, however good the object might be, and at last she planted her foot squarely against it.

Now I hate family breaches, and so didn't talk back much, although I kept back considerable. But she has such an aggressive way with her, that she finally convinced me that it was wrong for husbands to have or do anything that their wives didn't know all about. I acknowledged the justice of her remarks, and promised never to attend another lodge meeting again.

But Emily Jane is very aggressive, and was not disposed to let matters rest even there. She began upon me for the purpose of filching from me the secrets of the order. Of course I objected; every good Mason would do that; but every good Mason hasn't Emily Jane for a wife; I wish they had.

I held out for a long time, but, like a rat and a terrier, the harder I held out the harder she held on, until at last I agreed, for the sake of peace in the family, to expose the whole thing to her, while from fear that she might herself some day become a Mason (for in this age of progressive women, who knows what may not happen), I was afraid to diverge one jot from the truth, as every good Mason will see who follows up this *exposé*.

I began with her at the beginning, and am afraid the reader will have to do the same thing. But here it is, something as it was given me, and just as I gave it to my wife:

My Dear:—I was young when they took me in, and, like other youths possessing a little money and a festive turn of mind, I wanted to see and learn all about everything. That is how I came to get married, my dear—I—I beg pardon; it was love. Yes, unadulterated love.

Well, it would seem that the fraternity knew of my inclination, for they managed, in one way and another, to keep my curiosity up to a boiling point, and gave me to understand that I would be looked upon quite as favourably after I had become a Mason as I would be were I a member of the Young Men's Christian Association. Be a Mason! Guess I would, I thought.

I had heard they used people rather rough, and I asked several of those who had been put through the mill how the old thing worked, and they said, splendidly; that it was just as good as a wedding, and advised me to take it in by all means. So I went for the mysteries.

A committee of the whole took it into their heads to interview me as regards character, &c. Of course I knew what that meant, and so treated them to a champagne supper. They made an unanimous report in my favour, and the master of torture was directed to go for me at the next regular meeting.

Before the time appointed for the meeting arrived, I was notified by letter of my fate, and my friend Jenks came to volunteer his services in seeing me through the first degree. I am sure I was very much obliged to Jenks; but the air of sympathy and condolence which he wore made me feel a trifle shaky on my understanding.

I promised to return in a moment, and, without loss of time, I made my way to the nearest life insurance company and took out a heavy accident policy. You see I didn't know what might happen, and as I had *you* in my mind's eye, I had the policy made payable to you in case I found myself unable to collect it.

Thus backed up, I took my pilot's arm, and started for the lodge-room. In the ante-room I was introduced to several influential people, all of whom, without a single exception, smiled good-naturedly or otherwise, and expressed a hope that I should " get through safe."

This did not tend to quiet my nerves much, if any, and when I saw the brothers talking in groups and pointing over their shoulders at me with their thumbs, and heard the tickled laughs which they let escape them, I began to grow suspicious that the concern was even worse than the Sons of Malta, of which order I had some time before been made a member.

I asked Jenks if it wouldn't be a good idea to " take something" before the performance commenced. But he looked horrified, and said that I should not only be in danger of instant ejection, but might get roughly handled if the smell of liquor was discovered on me. He said the order was strictly temperate, and the thing would never do.

But I managed to get a smell at my bottle of hartshorn before the chief inquisitor came for me, and concluded to go it blind, and on an empty stomach. I say " concluded to "—in fact, I had no other alternative but to do so; for it seemed to be an understood thing that I was to suffer it all with my nerves uncovered.

The brethren gradually withdrew into the lodge-room, and I soon found myself alone with three or four savage-looking men, who appeared to eye me very much as a wolf would look upon a lamb in the same situation.

I spoke cheerfully regarding the weather and the prospect of good crops; but before either of them had a chance to reply, the door opened, and one of the brothers ordered more coal, adding that it was not half hot enough yet. My heart stopped to listen with my ears. Was that extra coal called for on my account?

" Haven't we but *one* to-night?" asked another charitable brother, putting his mouth to the wicket of the lodge-room door.

" That's all," was the cheerful reply.

Good gracious! I wish there had been a dozen, for misery loves company.

I was kept in this agony for a few moments, when my guards ordered me into an ante-room to strip. I felt bold; of course I did; and if I hadn't, I was the last person in the world to let them know it. If they were about to test my bravery, they should find it quite strong enough to satisfy them. So I stripped, and was given a pair of leather breeches, on many parts of which I observed strong straps or handles.

They laughed and talked while this was going on, and seemed excessively pleased at how hard Jones took it; saying that he fainted away under the operation, and was still in the hospital, while his friends mourned him as dead. This was very entertaining indeed, and I wondered if the lessons I had taken in club-swinging would be of any service to me now.

Before I had fairly settled it in my mind, the ruthless marauders rushed in upon me. Without so much as asking my pardon, they threw me upon a board about six feet in length, and lashed me securely to it. I asked one of them if that was "regular," and he replied by stuffing my mouth full of cayenne pepper. I was sneezing after that, and not asking many questions.

After lashing me securely to this board, they placed a pair of red goggles over my eyes and stood me up against the wall. They then told the doorkeeper that they were ready. Just then the door opened, and another brother came from the lodge-room, saying that there wasn't half fire enough yet. But I was in for it, and had quite enough to do to get used to my mouthful of pepper.

I heard somebody shovelling coal, and just as I began to perspire freely, I was seized by four strong men, lifted to their shoulders, where I rested for a moment—one of the most sensational moments of my life. My red goggles gave everybody the appearance of devils, and everything the appearance of being on fire, and red hot at that.

One of them commenced kicking at the lodge-room door, when somebody asked what the row was. Another of my friends began to talk back, although I hadn't the slightest idea what it was all about. But they seemed to settle it between them somehow, and then started with me for the interior of somewhere.

I could see just enough through my red goggles to convince me that I was among a rough lot, and that they intended to go for my very marrow. They toted me around the room for some time, stopping before each officer just long enough to give him a chance to indulge in a little pleasantry at my expense. Mr. Boss Mason looked at my teeth, and then filled my mouth with carpet-tacks. His first assistant felt of my pulse, took the measure of my feet, and daubed some tar on my nose. The second assistant put shoemaker's wax in my ears, and mashed me over the head with a claw-hammer.

Then I was handed around to the brethren, and each one went for me in his own particular way; after which I was placed face downward upon the floor, and the four men who had been passing me around sat down to rest upon the board to which I was lashed. Talk about times that try men's souls, this was trying to both soul and body. But they sang a hymn and chanted something about charity, which I thought they were not practising.

After they had become rested they again picked me up and carried me to a corner of the room, where the board to which I was lashed was fixed upright in strong centre-points at each end, and I was slowly turned before a red-hot stove, just as they turn a pig on a spit. The brethren gathered around and sang another cheerful hymn about the red-hot hereafter, just as though any place could be hotter than the one I was then in. The chief cook stood with a large sponge filled with kerosene oil, and every time I was turned away from the fire, as I went round and round, he would sponge me down and ask me if I felt like saying anything about it.

I told him it was all right; that he could rely on my secrecy for any length of time, but that I felt as though I was done on *one* side, and asked how long it would probably be before the order of exercises would change.

"Souse him!" exclaimed the Boss; and I was taken from the spit, and thrown into a huge tank filled with water, and told to swim for my life.

"How could I swim?" You may well ask that. Of course I couldn't, being lashed to that board; but they explained, after turning me over on my back once or twice for me to catch my breath, that this was intended to show me how valuable a thing it was to enjoy the advantages of a life-preserver; that I must see for myself that I should in all probability sink to the bottom had it not been for the float to which they had so kindly lashed me. They told me not to forget it, and I never shall.

APPENDIX.

After washing me off thoroughly, the Boss told them to take me out and arrange my toilet, after which the real initiation would be commenced. I was sure that they couldn't do worse than they had done, and so took heart when I heard the order given. But if this was Masonry, what was " roughing it?"

They assisted me to take off my goggles and leather breeches, and a little darkey, kept for the purpose, rubbed me down, and demanded a quarter for the job. I was told to spit out the carpet-tacks, which had evidently been given me to prevent my asking impertinent questions, since I could only articulate with the greatest difficulty, after which they assisted me into a shirt, a pair of boots, and, after securely blindfolding me, into a bonnet that had evidently been a bonnet for a long time.

I ventured to ask one of the brothers, who stood waiting for me, if everything thus far had been done regularly, and he said yes; that what I had thus far gone through was to quiet my nerves and give me an idea of what was coming. I thanked him for his information, and extended my hand in a friendly way, when he seized me by the arms from behind, and rushed me towards the lodge-room again.

At the door I was met by the First Assistant Boss, who pulled my nose and asked me how that was for high. This, he said, was to warn me, and to teach me, never to go anywhere hoodwinked; and, knowing how it was myself, never to be guilty of pulling a brother Mason's nose unless he refused to lend me money. We shook hands over it, and he proposed that we take a trip Down East.

We approached the Boss Mason.

"Put him in due posish!" he howled, as he saw us approach.

I was hustled into the centre of the room, made to stand on one leg, throwing the other out behind so as to make a carpenter's square of myself. The Boss approached me.

"Benighted outsider, you are now standing on the Geological Map of the Universe, your right toe pointing to the moon; and the stars are looking on without winking. How many fingers am I holding up?"

"Twelve, Boss, as near as I can see," I replied.

"Correct. This teaches you to always speak the truth. By-the-way, have you got such a thing as a shilling about you?"

"Nary a red, Boss."

"Spoken like a Mason. This is to teach you to look out for your loose change. Can you swear?"

"Like a trooper, Boss."

"Place him in due posish."

They placed me on the broad of my back, and gave me a speaking-trumpet.

"Now, then," said the Boss, "repeat after me, using the trumpet that all the brethren may hear you:

"THE FEARFUL FIRST OATH.

"I, Bricktop, in the presence of the best lot of men that ever lived, promise and swear, so help me Bob, that I will never go back on a poor Apprentice Boy; that while I am one myself I will cheerfully carry the hod for Master Masons; that I will always treat them when I meet them outside, or pilot them to a place where they keep a slate; that I will never make serious love to any gal on which a brother Apprentice is spoony; binding myself in three-hundred-dollar bonds to keep the peace, and never say a word about this night's proceedings, under the penalty of having my nose pulled by every member of the brotherhood wherever he may find me, and being obliged to drink alone and pay cash for it. Domino!"

"Double six!" (response by the brethren.)

Boss.—Keno.

Brethren.—Korrect!

Boss.—Let him arise and repeat the oath backwards from memory. If he misses a single word, off with his head, and salt him for the army.

Of course I did my best to save my head; but, after making an awful mess of it, I told them that I gave it up; that if my head was of any more use to them than it was to me, they were at liberty to take it.

APPENDIX.

The Boss then owned up that they were only fooling with me, but that it was to teach me a great moral lesson, never to take back anything I had once said, especially to a brother Mason. I remarked, "All right," and the Boss ordered the entertainment to go on.

They had several other great lessons to teach me, they said, and so went for me again. The Boss had in the meantime refilled his meerschaum, and after lighting it by digging the fire out of the Book-keeper's dudeen, he threw himself back in his chair, and shouted, "Go for him!"

The First Assistant Boss leaped from his seat, seized a ten-pound Indian club, and swinging it in such a manner as to strike me on that portion of my body usually allotted to chairs and benches, he managed to "raise" me fully three feet from the floor.

"That is given to teach you never to be caught without being *upholstered*," said the club-swinger, throwing down his weapon and returning to his seat.

As I succeeded in gathering myself up again, the Second Assistant came and asked me what I wanted most. I told him I wanted to see it out.

"Pose him and proceed!" shouted the Boss.

Several of them reached for me again, and I was placed in a sitting posture in the centre of the room. There was something dangerous going on, I felt sure, but I couldn't see what it was.

"Now, then," shouted the Boss, "let all bear a hand and give him the popular modern light."

Some kind brother struck a match, and held it under my nostrils just long enough to give me a taste of what was coming. Then another removed the hoodwink from my eyes, and I found myself surrounded by about a dozen men, each one engaged in filling a lighted kerosene lamp.

My nerves had become pretty tough by this time, or I could never have kept my position while this popular practice was going on. But I instantly took in the situation, and concluded that I could stand it if they could.

"This is to teach you never to contribute to newspaper items by attempting to fill a kerosene lamp with 'Non-explosive' oil. Arise!"

I arose.

"Stand erect."

I erected.

The Boss approached me from Down East.

"I am now about to give you the grip of an Apprentice Boy. Place your back against mine."

I calmly went back on him.

"Now, touch your elbows against mine, thus."

I bore my elbows against his'n.

"Now straighten up until your head touches mine."

I straightened up and touched.

"Is he all right, brother Assistant?"

"All right, Boss."

Just then I received a violent kick on the shins from the heel of the Boss, which made me draw up and take a step or two forward.

"This, my brother, is the grip of the Apprentice Boy. Of course you see it can be given anywhere without attracting the attention of the uninitiated. Brother Assistant, what do you call this part of the initiation?"

"The Apprentice Boy's Back Action Salutation, and is to teach the novice that extremes often meet."

"How shall he make himself known to, or ascertain if a stranger is on the square?"

"By approaching him from behind, and kicking his shins smartly. If he will stand that he is undoubtedly a square man, and will know that you are."

"Is it then safe to approach him?"

"That depends upon how good a Mason he is."

"What words belong to this degree?"

"There are two."

"Give them to me,"

" 'Keno.'

" 'Correct.' "

"These two words you will guard with jealous care. They are never used except between Apprentice Boys who wish to be sure of one another's identity, and only on great and important occasions."

I bowed in token of appreciation.

"Brother Assistant, what tools belong to this degree?"

"There are three, Boss; the Pick, Shovel, and Hod."

"What use is made of the Pick?"

"It is used in getting into hard places, and levelling things."

"What use is made of the Shovel?"

"It is used for scooping in; and the Hod is used to carry off what is made by the operation."

"What is the Apron for?"

"To keep your clothes clean; for it is the duty of every good Mason to show no traces of his business on his clothes."

"Correct. Brother, it will be your duty, at your earliest convenience, to get a showy brass emblem representing these tools, and wear it conspicuously about your person, that the world may see that you are one of 'em. You will now be taken back to the ante-room and clothed in your usual style, after which my Third Assistant will show you how to enter a lodge."

In about ten minutes I was back again, receiving my instructions.

"Provided you cannot smuggle yourself in," said my instructor, "you will approach the doorkeeper, and kick his shins. You will then say, '*Ke*,' and he will reply, '*No.*' *Keno*. If he is satisfied after this that you are a Mason, he will admit you. You will then approach the centre of the lodge-room, and there stand on your right leg, as you did while being examined by the Boss, and remain there until you catch his eye, when, if he thinks you are regular made, he will say, 'Correct,' and you are at liberty to be seated with the brethren. That's all."

The brethren now concluded their labours, and adjourned to the nearest refreshment saloon—at my expense.

END OF THE FIRST DEGREE.

MY WATCH.

A STORY BY MARK TWAIN.

My beautiful new watch had run· eighteen months without losing or gaining, and without breaking any part of its machinery or stopping. I had come to believe it infallible in its judgments about the time of day, and to consider its constitution and its anatomy imperishable. But at last, one night, I let it run down. I grieved about it as if it were a recognised messenger and forerunner of calamity. But, by-and-by, I cheered up, set the watch by guess, and commanded my bodings and superstitions to depart. Next day I stepped into the chief jeweller's to set it by exact time, and the head of the establishment took it out of my hands, and proceeded to set it for me. Then he said, "She is four minutes slow—regulator wants to be pushed up."

I tried to stop him—to make him understand that the watch kept perfect time. But no; all his human cabbage could see was that the watch was four minutes slow, and the regulator must be pushed up a little; and so, while I danced round him in anguish and beseeched him to let it alone, he calmly and cruelly did the shameful deed. My watch began to gain. It gained faster day by day. Within the week it sickened to a raging fever, and its pulse went up to a hundred and fifty in the shade. At the end of two months it had left all the timepieces of the town far in the rear, and was a fraction over thirteen days ahead of the almanac. It was away in November enjoying the snow, while the October leaves were still turning. It hurried up house-rent, bills payable, and such things in such a ruinous way that I could not abide by it. I took it to the watchmaker to be regulated. He asked me if I had ever had it repaired. I said no, it had never needed any repairing. He looked a look of vicious happiness and eagerly pried the watch open, then put a small dice-box into his eye and peered in its machinery. He said it wanted cleaning and oiling, besides regulating—come in a week.

APPENDIX. 103

After being cleaned and oiled and regulated, my watch slowed down to that degree that it ticked like a tolling bell. I began to be left by trains, I failed of all my appointments, I got to missing my dinner, my watch strung out three days grace to four, and let me go to protest; I gradually drifted back into yesterday, then day before, then into last week, and, by-and-by, the comprehension came upon me that all solitary and alone I was lingering along into week before last, and the world was out of sight. I seemed to detect in myself a sort of sneaking fellow-feeling for the mummy in the museum, and a desire to swap news with him. I went to the watchmaker again. He took the watch all to pieces while I waited, and then he said the barrel was "swelled." He said he could reduce it in three days. After this the watch averaged well, but nothing more. For half a day it would go like the very mischief, and keep up such a barking, and wheezing, and whooping, and sneezing, and snorting, that I could not hear myself think for the disturbance; and as long as it held out there was not a watch in the land that stood any chance against it. But the rest of the day it would keep on slowing down and fooling along, until all the clocks it had left behind caught up again.

So at last, at the end of twenty-four hours, it would trot up to the judge's stand all right and just on time. It would show a fair and square average, and no man could say it had done more or less than its duty. But a correct average is not only a mild virtue in a watch, and I took the instrument to another watchmaker. He said the king-bolt was broken. I said I was glad it was nothing more serious. To tell the plain truth, I had no idea what the king-bolt was, but I did not choose to appear ignorant to a stranger. He repaired the king-bolt, but what the watch gained in one way it lost in another. It would run a while, and then run a while longer, and so on using its own discretion about the intervals. And every time it kicked back like a musket.

I padded my breast for a few days, but finally took the watch to another watchmaker. He picked it all over to pieces and turned the ruin over and over under his glass; and then said there seemed to be something the matter with the hair-trigger. He fixed it and gave it a fresh start. It did well now, except that always at ten minutes to ten the hands would shut together in a pair of scissors, and from that time forth they would traverse together. The oldest man in the world could not make head nor tail to the time of day by such a watch, and so I went again to have the thing repaired. This person said that the crystal had got bent, and the main-spring was not straight. He also remarked that part of the works needed half-soling.

He made these things all right, and then my time-piece performed exceptionably, save that now and then, after working along quietly for nearly eight hours, everything inside would let go all of a sudden, and begin to spin round and round so fast that their individuality was lost completely and they simply seemed a delicate spider's web over the face of the watch. She would reel off the next twenty-four hours in six or seven minutes, then stop with a bang. I went with a heavy heart to one more watchmaker, and looked on while he took her to pieces. Then I prepared to cross-question him rigidly, for this was getting serious. The watch had cost two hundred dollars originally, and I seemed to have paid out two or three thousand for repairs. While I waited and looked, I presently recognised in this watchmaker an old acquaintance—a steamboat engineer of other days, and not a good engineer either. He examined all the parts carefully, just as the other watchmakers had done, and then delivered his verdict with the same confidence of manner.

He said, "She makes too much steam—you want to hang the monkey-wrench on the safety-valve!"

I brained him on the spot and had him buried at my own expense.

My Uncle William (now deceased, alas!) used to say that a good horse was a good horse until it had run away once, and that a good watch was a good watch until the repairer got a chance at it. And he used to wonder what became of all the unsuccessful tinkers and gunsmiths, and shoemakers and blacksmiths, but nobody could ever tell him.

THE HEATHEN CHINEE.

BY BRET HARTE.

WHICH I wish to remark,—
And my language is plain,—
That for ways that are dark
And for tricks that are vain,
The heathen Chinee is peculiar.
Which the same I would rise to explain.

Ah Sin was his name;
And I shall not deny
In regard to the same
What that name might imply,
But his smile it was pensive and childlike,
As I frequent remarked to Bill Nye.

It was August the third;
And quite soft was the skies;
Which it might be inferred
That Ah Sin was likewise;
Yet he played it that day upon William
And me in a way I despise.

Which we had a small game,
And Ah Sin took a hand:
It was Euchre. The same
He did not understand;
But he smiled as he sat by the table,
With the smile that was childlike and bland.

Yet the cards they were stocked
In a way that I grieve,
And my feelings were shocked
At the state of Nye's sleeve:
Which was stuffed full of aces and bowers,
And the same with intent to deceive.

But the hands that were played
  By that heathen Chinee,
And the points that he made,
  Were quite frightful to see,—
Till at last he put down a right bower,
  Which the same Nye had dealt unto me.

Then I looked up at Nye,
  And he gazed upon me;
And he rose with a sigh,
  And said " Can this be?
We are ruined by Chinese cheap labor,"—
  And he went for that heathen Chinee.

In the scene that ensued
  I did not take a hand,
But the floor it was strewed
  Like the leaves on the strand
With the cards that Ah Sin had been hiding,
  In the game " he did not understand."

In his sleeves, which were long,
  He had twenty-four packs,—
Which was coming it strong,
  Yet I state but the facts;
And we found on his nails, which were taper,
  What is frequent in tapers,—that's wax.

Which is why I remark,
  And my language is plain,
That for ways that are dark,
  And for tricks that are vain,
The heathen Chinee is peculiar,—
  Which the same I am free to maintain.

EPIGRAM.

BY GEORGE FRANCIS TRAIN.
(*Candidate for President.*)

THE BUGLE CALL.

HELP! oh help! my country save!
Follow your leader; down with fraud!
Be my partner, not party's slave,
God be with you! Praise the Lord.
    Wake up people! Death to Kings.
    Hallelujah! Smash the Rings.

No dead heads to church or press,
Immense mass-meetings everywhere,
Corruptionists in great distress;
Preachers engaged in prayer.
    Wake up people! Smash the Rings.
    Hallelujah! Death to Kings.

Off guns! out flags! ring bells; shout Hosannah.
Rise, boys! run a little faster,
Help me save our noble banner;
Help me smash the party plaster.
    Wake up people! Death to Kings.
    Hallelujah! Break the Rings.

While editors and politicians sneer,
At earthquake's change in seventy-two,
The volcan' action of a people's cheer
Shows that the nation's heart is true.
    Hallelujah! Death to Kings.
    Wake up voters! Smash the Rings.

Hear that spiritual army ; hark!
Death to hypocrite, thief, and liar!
Peter the Hermit! Joan of Arc!
Cleanse the stables with prairie fire.
    Wake up people ! Down with Kings.
    Hallelujah ! Smash the Rings.

The storm is passing ; hail the sun ;
The rainbow circles all the sky.
Man's God-like race is not yet run ;
Virtue decrees that vice must die.
    Hallelujah ! Smash the Rings.
    Wake up people ! Death to Kings.

Official rats you see are running :
Fire the *Revolution* gun ;
Clear the track! the TRAIN is coming,
The Reformation has begun.
    Wake up people ! Death to Kings.
    Hallelujah ! Smash the Rings.

$20
BOND.
No. 230.
—
ISSUED TO

....

DATE OF SUBSCRIPTION.

..........186

No. 230.

No. 1771.

IT IS HEREBY CERTIFIED that

THE IRISH REPUBLIC

is indebted unto.................................or bearer, in the sum of TWENTY DOLLARS, redeemable Six Months after the acknowledgement of the Independence of the Irish Nation, with interest from the date hereof, inclusive, at Six per cent. per annum, payable on presentation of this bond at Treasury of the Irish Republic.

JOHN OSNABURG,
Agent for the Irish Republic.

..............186

A FENIAN BOND.

LONDON:
PRINTED BY WILLIAM CLOWES AND SONS,
STAMFORD STREET AND CHARING CROSS.

www.ingramcontent.com/pod-product-compliance
Lightning Source LLC
Chambersburg PA
CBHW022144160426
43197CB00009B/1423